♋   THE CANCER ENIGMA   ♋

Cracking the Code

ALSO BY JANE RIDDER-PATRICK

A Handbook of Medical Astrology
Shaping Your Future (Series of 12 titles)
Shaping Your Relationships (Series of 12 titles)

The Zodiac Code series

THE
CANCER
ENIGMA

Cracking the Code

JANE RIDDER-PATRICK

MAINSTREAM
PUBLISHING
EDINBURGH AND LONDON

For my son Alleyne, with love

First published in Great Britain in 2004 by
MAINSTREAM PUBLISHING COMPANY
(EDINBURGH) LTD
7 Albany Street
Edinburgh EH1 3UG

ISBN 978 1 84018 530 0

A catalogue record for this book is available
from the British Library

Typeset in Allise and Van Dijck

Penguin Random House is committed to a sustainable future for
our business, our readers and our planet. This book is made from
Forest Stewardship Council® certified paper.

MIX
Paper from
responsible sources
FSC® C018179

Printed and bound in Great Britain by Clays Ltd, Elcograf S.p.A.

Contents

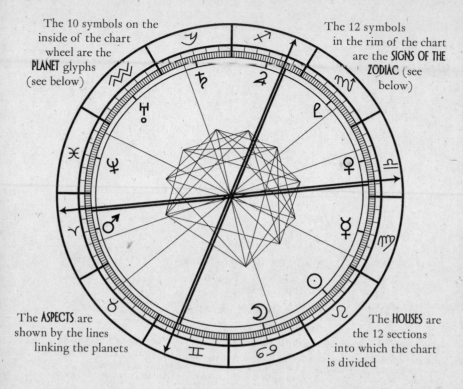

The 10 symbols on the inside of the chart wheel are the **PLANET** glyphs (see below)

The 12 symbols in the rim of the chart are the **SIGNS OF THE ZODIAC** (see below)

The **ASPECTS** are shown by the lines linking the planets

The **HOUSES** are the 12 sections into which the chart is divided

A Sample Birth Chart

Sign	Ruler	Sign	Ruler
Aries ♈	Mars ♂	Libra ♎	Venus ♀
Taurus ♉	Venus ♀	Scorpio ♏	Pluto ♇
Gemini ♊	Mercury ☿	Sagittarius ♐	Jupiter ♃
Cancer ♋	Moon ☽	Capricorn ♑	Saturn ♄
Leo ♌	Sun ☉	Aquarius ♒	Uranus ♅
Virgo ♍	Mercury ☿	Pisces ♓	Neptune ♆

ONE

The Truth of Astrology

MOST PEOPLE'S FIRST EXPERIENCE OF ASTROLOGY IS THROUGH newspapers and magazines. This is a mixed blessing for astrology's reputation — writing an astrology column to any degree of accuracy is a tough, many would say impossible, challenge. The astrologer has to try to say something meaningful about conditions that affect every single person belonging to the same sign, over a very short period of time, in a scant handful of words. The miracle is that some talented astrologers do manage to get across a tantalising whiff of the real thing and keep readers coming back for more of what most of us are hungry for — self-knowledge and reassurance about the future. The downside of the popularity of these columns is that many people think that all astrology is a branch of the entertainment industry and is limited to light-hearted fortune-telling. This is far from the truth.

What Astrology Can Offer

Serious astrology is one of the most sophisticated tools available to help us understand ourselves and the world around us. It gives us a language and a framework to examine and describe – quite literally – *anything* under the Sun, from countries to companies, from money markets to medical matters. Its most common application, however, is in helping people to understand themselves better using their own unique birth charts. Astrology has two main functions. One is to describe the traits and tendencies of whatever it is that is being examined, whether this is a state, a software company or someone's psyche. The other is to give an astonishingly accurate timetable for important changes within that entity. In the chapters that follow, we'll be using astrology to investigate the psychology of the innermost part of your personality, taking a look at what drives, inspires and motivates you.

Astrology uses an ancient system of symbols to describe profound truths about the nature of life on earth, truths that cannot be weighed and measured, but ones we recognise nevertheless, and that touch and move us at a deep level. By linking mythology and mathematics, astrology bridges the gap between our inner lives and our outer experiences, between mind and matter, between poetry and science.

Fate and Free Will

Some people think that astrology is all about foretelling the future, the implication being that everything is predestined and that we have no say in how our lives take shape. None of that is true. We are far from being helpless victims of fate. Everything that happens to us at any given time is the result of past choices. These choices may have been our own, or made by other people. They could even have been made long ago before we, or even our grandparents, were born. It is not always possible to prevent processes that were set in motion in the past from coming to their logical conclusions as events that we then have to deal with. We are, however, all free to decide how to react to whatever is presented to us at every moment of our lives.

Your destiny is linked directly with your personality because the choices you make, consciously or unconsciously, depend largely on your own natural inclinations. It is these inclinations that psychological astrology describes. You can live out every single part of your chart in a constructive or a less constructive way. For instance, if you have Aries strong in your chart, action and initiative will play a major role in your life. It is your choice whether you express yourself aggressively or assertively, heroically or selfishly, and also whether you are the doer or the done-to. Making the right choices is important because every decision has consequences – and what you give out, sooner or later, you get back. If you don't know and understand yourself, you are 'fated' to act according to instinct and how your life experiences have conditioned you. By revealing how you are wired up temperamentally, astrology can highlight alternatives to blind knee-jerk reactions, which often make existing problems worse. This self-knowledge can allow you to make more informed free-will choices, and so help you create a better and more successful future for yourself.

Astrology and Prediction

Astrology cannot predict specific events based on your birth chart. That kind of prediction belongs to clairvoyance and divination. These specialities, when practised by gifted and responsible individuals, can give penetrating insights into events that are likely to happen in the future if matters proceed along their present course.

The real benefit of seeing into the future is that if we don't like what could happen if we carry on the way we're going, we can take steps either to prevent it or to lessen its impact. Rarely is the future chiselled out in stone. There are many possible futures. What you feed with your attention grows. Using your birth chart, a competent astrologer can map out, for years in advance, major turning points, showing which areas of your life will be affected at these times and the kind of change that will be taking place. This information gives answers to the questions that most clients ask in one way or another: 'Why me, why this and why now?' If you accept responsibility for facing what needs to be done at the appropriate time, and doing it, you can change the course of your life for the better.

Astrology and the Soul

What is sometimes called the soul and its purpose is a mystery much more profound than astrology. Most of us have experienced 'chance' meetings and apparent 'tragedies' which have affected the direction of our entire lives. There is an intelligence at work that is infinitely wiser and more powerful than the will or wishes of our small egocentric personalities. This force, whatever name we give it – Universal Wisdom, the Inner Guide, the Self, a guardian angel – steers us into exactly the right conditions for our souls' growth. Astrology can pinpoint the turning points in the course of your destiny and describe the equipment that you have at your disposal for serving, or resisting, the soul's purpose. That equipment is your personality.

Who Are You?

You are no doubt aware of your many good qualities as well as your rather more resistible ones that you might prefer to keep firmly under wraps. Maybe you have wondered why it is that one part of your personality seems to want to do one thing while another part is stubbornly intent on doing the exact opposite. Have you ever wished that you could crack the code that holds the secrets of what makes you – and significant others – behave in the complex way you do? The good news is that you can, with the help of your astrological birth chart, sometimes known as your horoscope.

Just as surely as your DNA identifies you and distinguishes you from everyone else, as well as encoding your peculiarities and potential, your birth chart reveals the unique 'DNA fingerprinting' of your personality. This may seem a staggering claim, but it is one that those who have experienced serious astrology will endorse, so let's take a closer look at what a birth chart is.

Your Birth Chart

Your birth chart is a simplified diagram of the positions of the planets, as seen from the place of your birth, at the moment you took your first independent breath. Critics have said that astrology is obviously nonsense because birth charts are drawn up as if the Sun and all the planets moved round the Earth.

We know in our minds that the Earth moves round the Sun, but that doesn't stop us seeing the Sun rise in the east in the morning and move across the sky to set in the west in the evening. This is an optical illusion. In the same way, we know (or at least most of us know) that we are not really the centre of the universe, but that doesn't stop us experiencing ourselves as being at the focal point of our own personal worlds. It is impossible to live life in any other way. It is the strength, not weakness, of astrology that it describes from your own unique viewpoint how you, as an individual, experience life.

Erecting Your Chart

To draw up a full birth chart you need three pieces of information – the date, time and place of your birth. With your birth date alone you can find the positions of all the planets (except sometimes the Moon) to a good enough degree of accuracy to reveal a great deal of important information about you. If you have the time and place of birth, too, an astrologer can calculate your Ascendant or Rising Sign and the houses of your chart – see below. The Ascendant is a bit like the front door of your personality and describes your general outlook on life. (If you know your Ascendant sign, you might like to read more about its characteristics in the book on that sign in this series.)

The diagram on page 6 shows what a birth chart looks like. Most people find it pretty daunting at first sight but it actually breaks down into only four basic units – the planets, the signs, the aspects and the houses.

The Planets

Below is a simple list of what the planets represent.

PLANET	REPRESENTS YOUR URGE TO
☉ The Sun	express your identity
☽ The Moon	feel nurtured and safe
☿ Mercury	make connections
♀ Venus	attract what you love
♂ Mars	assert your will
♃ Jupiter	find meaning in life
♄ Saturn	achieve your ambitions
♅ Uranus	challenge tradition
♆ Neptune	serve an ideal
♇ Pluto	eliminate, transform and survive

The planets represent the main psychological drives that every single one of us has. The exact way in which we express these drives is not fixed from birth but develops and evolves throughout our lives, both consciously and unconsciously. In this book we will be examining in detail four of these planets — your Sun, Moon, Mercury and Venus. These are the bodies that are right at the heart of our solar system. They correspond, in psychological astrology, to the core of your personality and represent how you express yourself, what motivates you emotionally, how you use your mind and what brings you pleasure.

The Signs
The signs your planets are in show how you tend to express your inner drives. For example, if your Mars is in the action sign of Aries, you will assert yourself pretty directly, pulling no punches. If your Venus is in secretive Scorpio, you will attract, and also be attracted to, emotionally intense relationships. There is a summary of all of the signs on p. 128.

The Aspects
Aspects are important relationships between planets and whether your inner characteristics clash with or complement each other depends largely on whether or not they are in aspect and whether that aspect is an easy or a challenging one. In Chapter Six we'll be looking at some challenging aspects to the Sun.

The Houses
Your birth chart is divided into 12 slices, called houses, each of which is associated with a particular area of life, such as friendships, travel or home life. If, for example, you have your Uranus in the house of career, you are almost

certainly a bit of a maverick at work. If you have your Neptune in the house of partnership, you are likely to idealise your husband, wife or business partner.

The Nature of Time

Your birth chart records a moment in time and space, like a still from a movie — the movie being the apparent movement of the planets round the earth. We all know that time is something that can be measured in precise units, which are always the same, like seconds, months and centuries. But if you stop to reflect for a moment, you'll also recognise that time doesn't always feel the same. Twenty minutes waiting for a bus on a cold, rainy day can seem like a miserable eternity, while the same amount of time spent with someone you love can pass in a flash. As Einstein would say — that's relativity.

There are times in history when something significant seems to be in the air, but even when nothing momentous is happening the quality of time shifts into different 'moods' from moment to moment. Your birth chart is impregnated with the qualities of the time when you were born. For example, people who were born in the mid-to-late 1960s, when society was undergoing major disruptive changes, carry those powerful energies within them and their personalities reflect, in many ways, the turmoil of those troubled and exciting times. Now, as adults, the choices that those individuals make, based on their own inner conflicts and compulsions, will help shape the future of society for better or worse. And so it goes on through the generations.

Seed Meets Soil

There is no such thing as a good or bad chart, nor is any one sign better or worse than another. There are simply 12 different, but equally important, life focuses. It's useful to keep in mind the fact that the chart of each one of us is made up of all the signs of the zodiac. This means that we'll act out, or experience, *every* sign somewhere in our lives. It is true, however, that some individual charts are more challenging than others; but the greater the challenge, the greater the potential for achievement and self-understanding.

In gardening terms, your chart is a bit like the picture on a seed packet. It shows what you could become. If the seeds are of poppies, there's no way you'll get petunias, but external conditions will affect how they grow. With healthy soil, a friendly climate and green-fingered gardeners, the plants have an excellent chance of flourishing. With poor soil, a harsh climate or constant neglect, the seeds will be forced to struggle. This is not always a disadvantage. They can become hardy and adapt, finding new and creative ways of evolving and thriving under more extreme conditions than the plant that was well cared for. It's the same with your chart. The environment you were raised in may have been friendly or hostile to your nature and it will have done much to shape your life until now. Using the insights of astrology to affirm who you are, you can, as an adult, provide your own ideal conditions, become your own best gardener and live out more fully – and successfully – your own highest potential.

TWO

The Symbolism of Cancer

WE CAN LEARN A GREAT DEAL ABOUT CANCER BY LOOKING at the symbols, myths and legends associated with it. These are time-honoured ways of describing psychological truths; they carry more information than plain facts alone and hint at the deeper meanings and significance of the sign.

The Cancer glyph of two circles, with semi-circles attached, has been interpreted in many ways over the years. The circles, side by side, are said to represent breasts, while the semi-circles are arms, positioned as if supporting a baby. These arms symbolise the giving and receiving of nurture and protection. One is cupped to gather and collect, while the other is upturned to pour out its sustenance, showing the Cancerian need to have and to hold. The glyph also depicts a mother bending over and tending to her child. The doubling of the motif can be seen as two individuals – mother and infant – bound together in close relationship, yet also separate. The halves of the glyph seem to somersault over each other, hinting at the way the behaviour of Cancerians can flip over from motherly to childlike and back again. It shows too the periodic leaps of development that Cancerians make throughout their lives, yet always manage to cycle back to home base.

Cancer the Crab

The symbol for Cancer wasn't always a crab. For the ancient Egyptians, it was the scarab, or dung beetle. This, they believed, laid its eggs in a ball of dung that it then rolled along in front of it. The life cycle of the beetle mirrored the rebirth of the Sun at each new dawn, and its daily 'rolling' across the Heavens. Being symbols of creation, immortality and eternal renewal, precious scarab ornaments were once buried with the dead as amulets for resurrection in the next world. In Babylonian times, Cancer's animal was a tortoise, or turtle, which was associated with the Moon. It symbolised creative powers, fruitfulness and regeneration, as well as the passage of time, which is marked by the Moon's monthly cycles. The crab and the turtle are amphibious creatures, at home both on dry land and in water, just as Cancerians are equally at home in two worlds – in the subtle inner world of imagination and shifting feelings, and in the practical outer world of everyday responsibilities. Both have hard, protective shells that they retreat into at the first sign of danger, just like Cancerians – though your shell is emotional, in the form of a crusty defensiveness. The crab also sheds it shell periodically so that it can grow. To protect its vulnerability at these stages, it hides itself away until another shell develops. You too go through cycles of emotional growth and turmoil, during which you retreat from, and then return, strengthened, to the world.

Cancer in Myth and Legend

The crab appears in the second of the Twelve Labours of the hero Hercules. His task was to kill the Hydra, a hideous nine-headed serpent that lived in a swamp with its devoted friend, a large crab. The monster was destroying all the crops and animals in the neighbourhood and its breath was so toxic that it killed on impact. Hercules marched in with his usual boldness, but was soon in deep trouble. The Hydra wrapped its many necks around his feet and every time he chopped off a head another two grew in its place. The crab, at the request of the goddess Hera who hated Hercules, pitched in to help the Hydra, and started nipping at the hero's ankle. This nearly cost Hercules the battle. Eventually, however, the crab was crushed but Hera, as a reward for its help, raised it to the heavens in the constellation of Cancer. The myth shows several Cancerian traits, both positive and negative. If you are attached to someone, even a person that nobody else can stand, you'll stand by and protect them to the last – but often you don't look at the wider implications and consequences of your clannishness for the world at large.

The Constellation of Cancer

The constellation of Cancer, the least conspicuous in the zodiac, contains a cluster of stars known as the Praesaepe (the manger or crib), with two stars on either side known as the Aselli (the Asses), which carry all of the associations of Christ's humble birth in a stable. The ancients used these stars to predict the weather. If they weren't crystal clear, bad weather was likely to be on the way – in much the same way that emotional squalls are signalled when your face clouds over. The Chaldeans called the constellation of Cancer the 'Gate of Men', through which the soul

18

incarnates and spirit is made flesh. For all your shyness, you have a major role to play in giving birth to and fostering creative ventures, whether these are flesh-and-blood children, artistic works, caring projects or business enterprises.

The Ruler of Cancer

Each sign is associated with a planet, which is called its ruler, and the sign and its ruler have many common characteristics. Cancer is ruled by the Moon. The Moon depends for its light on a source outside of itself, the Sun. It then reflects this light on to Earth at night, the time of darkness and sleep. Like the Moon, you, as a Cancerian, pick up whatever sensations are around you, especially other people's needs and feelings. You can feel incomplete without someone or something else to cling to and into whom you can pour the light of your intuitive wisdom. The Moon is constantly changing, yet reliable and predictable within that cyclic change, just like you. At New Moon, the Moon is closest to the Sun and is completely invisible. Circling the Earth, it reaches the height of its powers at Full Moon, when it is furthest away from the Sun. At that time it sends maximum light to Earth, then goes on to complete its journey, when it forms the next New Moon. In the same way, you not only need to touch home base regularly for refuelling, but also, just as regularly, you need to separate from it in order to fulfil, and to give to the world, your highest creative potential.

The Season of Cancer

The sign of Cancer begins at the summer solstice, the longest day in the northern hemisphere and the shortest in the south. Traditionally, magic was said to be in the air then. Love potions were brewed and rituals performed for the health and fertility of the land, its people and its livestock. Wells and fountains were cleaned and decorated; bathing in their waters at midsummer was reputed to have special healing powers, as were herbs picked at that time. St John's Wort is supposed to flower on 24 June, St John's Day, and to have miraculous powers. Research has shown it to be an effective treatment for mild depression and anxiety — conditions that many Cancerians are prone to when feeling out of sorts.

THREE

The Heart of the Sun

O THE GLYPH FOR THE SUN IS A PERFECT CIRCLE WITH A DOT in the centre and symbolises our dual nature — earthly and eternal. The circle stands for the boundary of the personality, which distinguishes and separates each individual from every other individual, for it is our differences from other people that make us unique, not our similarities. The dot in the centre indicates the mysterious 'divine spark' within us and the potential for becoming conscious of who we truly are, where we have come from and what we may become.

The Meaning of the Sun

Each of your planets represents a different strand of your personality. The Sun is reckoned to be the most important factor of your whole birth chart. It describes your sense of identity, and the sign that the Sun was in when you were born, your Sun sign, along with its house position and any aspects to other planets, shows how you express and develop that identity.

Your Role in Life

Each of the signs is associated with certain roles that can be played in an infinite number of ways. Take one of the roles of Aries, which is the warrior. A warrior can cover anything from Attila the Hun, who devastated vast stretches of Europe with his deliberate violence, to an eco-warrior, battling to save the environment. The role, warrior, is the same; the motivation and actions are totally different. You can live out every part of your personality in four main ways – as creator, destroyer, onlooker or victim. How you act depends on who you choose to be from the endless variations possible from the symbolism of each of your planets, but most particularly your Sun. And you do have a choice; not all Geminis are irresponsible space cadets nor is every Scorpio a sex-crazed sadist. This book aims to paint a picture of what some of your choices might be and show what choices, conscious or unconscious, some well-known people of your sign have made.

Your upbringing will have helped shape what you believe about yourself and out of those beliefs comes, automatically, behaviour to match. For example, if you believe you are a victim, you will behave like one and the world will happily oblige by victimising you. If you see yourself as a carer, life will present you with plenty to care for – and often to care about, too. If you identify yourself as an adventurer, you'll spot opportunities at every corner. If you're a winner, then you'll tend to succeed. Shift the way that you see yourself and your whole world shifts, too.

Your Vocation

Your Sun describes your major life focus. This is not always a career. As the poet Milton said: 'They also serve who only stand and wait.' It is impossible to tell from your Sun sign exactly what your calling is – there are people of all signs occupied in practically every area of life. What is important is not so much *what* you do, but the way that you do it and it is this – how you express yourself – that your Sun describes. If you spend most of your time working at an occupation or living in a situation where you can't give expression to the qualities of your Sun, or which forces you to go against the grain of your Sun's natural inclinations, then you're likely to live a life of quiet, or possibly even noisy, desperation.

On Whose Authority

Your personality, which your birth chart maps, is like a sensitive instrument that will resonate only to certain frequencies – those that are similar to its own. Your Sun shows the kind of authority that will strike a chord with you, either positively or negatively, because it is in harmony with yours. It can show how you relate to people in authority, especially your father. (It is the Moon that usually shows the relationship with your mother and home.) In adult life it can throw light onto the types of bosses you are likely to come across, and also how you could react to them. It is a major part of the maturing process to take responsibility for expressing your own authority wisely. When you do so, many of your problems with external authorities diminish or even disappear.

In a woman's chart the Sun can also describe the kind of husband she chooses. This is partly because, traditionally, a husband had legal authority over his wife. It is also because, especially in the early years of a marriage, many women choose to pour their energies into homemaking and supporting their husbands' work in the world, rather than their own, and so his career becomes her career. As a

Cancerian, you may find that your father, boss or husband shows either the positive or negative traits of Cancer or, as is usually the case, a mixture of both – caring, sympathetic and intuitive or clingy, touchy and clannish.

Born on the Cusp

If you were born near the beginning or end of Cancer, you may know that your birthday falls on the cusp, or meeting point, of two signs. The Sun, however, can only be in one sign or the other. You can find out for sure which sign your Sun is in by checking the tables on pp. 97–8.

FOUR

The Drama of Being a Cancer

EACH SIGN IS ASSOCIATED WITH A CLUSTER OF ROLES THAT HAVE their own core drama or storyline. Being born is a bit like arriving in the middle of an ongoing play and slipping into a certain part. How we play our characters is powerfully shaped in early life by having to respond to the input of the other actors around us - the people that make up our families and communities. As the play of our lives unfolds, we usually become aware that there are themes which tend to repeat themselves. We may ask ourselves questions like 'Why do I always end up with all the work / caught up in fights / with partners who mistreat me / in dead-end jobs / successful but unhappy . . .?' or whatever. Interestingly, I've found that people are less likely to question the wonderful things that happen to them again and again.

The good news is that once we recognise the way we have been playing our roles, we can then use our free-will choice to do some creative rescripting, using the same character in more constructive scenarios. Even better news is that if we change, the other people in our dramas have got to make some alterations, too. If you refuse to respond to the same old cues in the customary ways, they are going to have to get creative too.

Whether you are male or female, your major themes as a Cancerian are Mother and Child. You can find yourself playing either one of these parts and even switch roles frequently. It's important to recognise that not all Cancerians are maternal in the narrow sense of the word. Many aren't even particularly fond of children. But you do need some creative project of your own to give birth to and to take under your wing and foster.

A mother's task is to look after her offspring. She may be caring and kind to others too, but her loyalty is, first and last, towards her own babes. She carries them through pregnancy, gives birth, then feeds, clothes and protects her young until they are independent enough to look after themselves – and then releases them out into the world. A nursing mother with full breasts experiences pain without a hungry baby to relieve her of the pressure of her milk. This bliss of mutual pleasure, satisfying a mutual need to give and to receive, shows Cancer at its best. Without someone or something vulnerable, yet full of potential, to nurture, protect and foster, you are incomplete.

While infants are tiny, they are vulnerable and dependent on mother for their very existence. This is an enormously powerful position, for if mother withholds her care the infant will die. This power can be misused: insecure Cancerians can apply emotional blackmail by threatening to withdraw love from those who depend on them, if their demands are not met. Another temptation for mother is to refuse to allow her offspring to lead independent lives and to try to bind them to her apron strings long past the time they should have been weaned and pushed out of the nest.

The other half of Cancer's drama is The Child, moving from a position of total dependence to the interdependence of adulthood. A baby's primary task is to survive. By tuning in to its mother's feelings, it quickly learns to manipulate the world to have its own requirements met. A child can be delightful but if allowed to dominate can also be a ruthless, demanding brat, resorting to sulks and tantrums if everything isn't exactly to its liking, immediately. The task for a growing child, like that of all Cancerians, is to develop a sense of fairness and responsibility towards others, without neglecting its own needs in the process.

The lives of most Cancerians are touched at some time by separation, actual or threatened, from mother, child, support system or a creative endeavour that you are attached to. This is usually the beginning of a new phase of maturity that you, periodically, are called – or forced – to go through. Just as the Moon, as it waxes, moves away from the Sun, you need to learn to let go of dependency, to grow and become a source of light to others and move on to your next cycle, trusting that support will be there for you when you need it.

How you choose to see your role will determine your behaviour. The following chapter describes some typical Cancerian behaviour. Remember, though, that there is no such thing as a person who is all Cancer and nothing but Cancer. You are much more complicated than that and other parts of your chart will modify, or may even seem to contradict, the single, but central, strand of your personality which is your Sun sign. These other sides of your nature will have their own roles in the drama that is you, adding colour and contrast and may restrict or reinforce your basic Cancer identity. They won't, however, cancel out the challenges you face as a Cancerian.

27

FIVE

The Cancer Temperament

CANCER IS A CARDINAL SIGN AND, LIKE ALL THOSE WHOSE SUN IS IN a cardinal sign, you have a goal. Yours is to direct, protect and provide for those you take under your wing. You are drawn to people and projects that are vulnerable, and therefore in need of your own special care and attention. You can see the potential for creative development that others overlook (and sometimes, on closer examination, still fail to find . . .).

Mother Knows Best
With quiet dedication and determination, you'll work away patiently, moulding and shaping your chosen labour of love, nudging and guiding and sometimes shaking it into shape, holding your vision of it as healthy and flourishing – and responsive to you. Often your ideas of what is right and possible are wise, shrewd and loving. Because your influence, although often subtle, is so powerful, you do have to be careful that you leave those in your care enough space to evolve according to their own natural inclinations, which may not always correspond with your idea of how things

should be. You may also expect, as your right, affection and gratitude for services rendered, and become a bit of a martyr when these — often unspoken — demands are not met. Nothing will alienate you more quickly from those you most want to be close to. The secret is to provide gladly with no thought of return, allowing others to become independent and learn from their own mistakes. When you do this, the tenderness, intimacy and sense of belonging that you shower on others, and need so much for yourself, comes back to you in abundance.

Letting Go

Once your offspring — whether this is a child, business or creative project — has an independent life of its own, it's important to find other outlets for your nurturing energy or you may be tempted to hold on, for fear that without it you'll hardly exist. Give in to that impulse, though, and you will stifle both it and yourself. A good mother works to make herself redundant. This can be a tough lesson, but letting go allows space for something new to come into your life.

Instinctive Wisdom

Being programmed to nurture and shelter, you are instantly aware of people's wants and feel moved to supply them. With your gifts of gentleness and affection, your heart and helping hands reach out instinctively to those in need of care and guidance. You can be the thread of gold that knits together the day-to-day steering of a family or a company, as you can respond promptly and sensitively to constantly changing situations and demands, providing what's required often before others even recognise the need in themselves. You respond immediately and often unconsciously to minute shifts in the emotional atmosphere. In modern civilisations, this natural sensitivity to the environment, which Cancerians have in a heightened form, is often a lost art. In one tribal community where nappies were never used and the mothers always seemed to know when their babies needed to relieve themselves of earth, wind or water, an anthropologist, puzzled, asked one of the women how she knew that evacuation was imminent. The woman answered, equally puzzled, that she knew in exactly the same way that she knew her own body required attention – didn't he?

Acute Sensitivity

As you are so very impressionable, you need to be careful about who you associate with, as you pick up their moods instantly. You can even mirror other people's body language and take on their tone of voice. As you feel everything so intensely, you tend to interpret all the sensations you are picking up from your own personal viewpoint, as if they were your own. In fact, frequently you may believe that they *are* your own. Some Cancerians experience fear and panic attacks, and even hallucinations, for no known reason. If you are one of those, it is worth checking out where you are, and with whom, when this occurs. The chances are they have nothing to do with you, and that you are simply tuning in to someone else's terrors and experiencing those for them. The art is to distinguish whose feelings it is you are feeling – then let go of those that are not your own. This is easier said than done, but once you've mastered it, you won't be at the mercy of your constantly changing feelings, tossed about like a cork on the ocean. You'll have a highly sophisticated radar system at your disposal, giving you valuable information about what is going on around, and inside, you.

Past Tense

You may have irrational likes and dislikes, triggered by deeply ingrained memories of events from the past. Like an elephant is reputed to, you never forget anything that has made an impression on your feelings. Some old memories are best left behind – especially ancient hurts and grudges and limiting beliefs. It is important that you recognise just how sensitive, receptive and vulnerable you are. Two of the biggest favours you can do to protect and care for yourself are to surround yourself with people who adore you, and to exclude as far as possible negative influences.

Deep and Reflective

Like a pond that reflects everything near it and accepts and contains all that goes into it, you sense and absorb all the moods, colours, movements and subtle atmospheres around you, soaking up joy and emotional junk alike. Sometimes you can reflect back unthinkingly, without checking the facts and ideas that are doing the rounds. The giveaway is when you start sentences with 'Everybody knows . . .' or 'They say . . .'. It's not always easy for you to analyse and talk about your feelings, as they can shift so quickly and be so many-layered and delicate, giving you a richly complex inner life. Reflecting on them, pondering and turning them over in your mind and heart until you understand them fully, transforms your experiences into wisdom. Then you can draw on your insights and express them through creativity of some kind – tuning in to the needs of a child, the movements of the markets or the atmospheres you convey by your art. Cancerian writers' work is often autobiographical and notable for capturing subtleties of mood.

Your Own Folk

Cancer is the sign of home and family and although you are sensitive to everyone you meet, you lavish your loving kindness mainly on those you consider to be your kith and kin, whether they are your own blood relatives or those you have chosen to take into your fold. You tend to divide the world into the black and white categories of 'us' and 'them', and see 'them' as, at best, suspect and, at worst, positively dangerous. After the 2001 terrorist attacks on New York, US President and Cancerian George W. Bush announced that those who weren't on the side of the US must be for the terrorists. You can be fiercely sentimental about preserving old family, community or national traditions, as you have a strong sense of lineage and of the responsibility to produce descendants. Probably, like most Cancerians, you are fascinated by your ancestral history because this gives you a feeling of continuity. It's important not to become too narrow in outlook, seeing life only from the viewpoint of your family or country, with little interest, tolerance or understanding of the world beyond your own familiar, but restricted, boundaries.

The Ever-Present Past

You find it hard to throw away mementoes of the past. To others this may look like just plain clutter, but those treasured photographs and letters, yellowing concert tickets, dog-eared receipts and disintegrating flowers from bouquets long withered are as important to you as a child's comfort blanket. They are reassuring reminders of a past which is known, safe and familiar. You can be anxious about the future, which is unknown, and therefore scary. As you want to be prepared for every eventuality, to waste not and want not, you'll tuck away whatever comes your way in boxes and bags and piles, under your bed, in cupboards and attics and cellars. Who knows when that tiny length of string or those ten pairs of worn-out socks will come in handy? Parting with the debris of your past – including old attitudes and hurts – can be a major trauma for many Cancerians. You prefer to acquire and stockpile and hoard. After all, why should you pay in the unknown land of the future for something you already have? Folk wisdom reminds you to 'Put your trust in God, but remember to lock your car'. It's the first part that you could do well to take to heart. Learning to trust life is hard, but every step you take in that direction will improve your sense of security and self-confidence.

Touchy Feely

You are hypersensitive to any threat of rejection and can take personally, and become touchy and offended by, remarks or looks that weren't even directed at you. You loathe being teased, but can be a relentless tease yourself. You may be superstitious, and carry around a vague, pessimistic suspicion of nameless dangers lurking. Your vivid imagination is skilled at conjuring up worst-case scenarios. If you've made a fool of yourself, waves of humiliation can overwhelm you, making you brood and fret in anguish. You close off when angry and can turn sullen, peevish and cantankerous. Your glacial withdrawals, heavy with unspoken accusation, can make everyone tiptoe round you, feeling guilty without being quite sure why, or what they're supposed to have done. If you feel wronged, you can become sulky and withdrawn, nursing your resentment into a full-blown grudge. This can tempt you to hit below the belt with bitchy little nips and veiled insults, or to rip people to pieces behind their backs, then smile at them sweetly when face to face.

Shell Suited

Being timid, you hate to expose yourself to risks, so you may build a protective shell of shyness and reserve around you. Some Cancerians, though, seem to go to the opposite extreme and behave as if they were wild extroverts. This is usually a smokescreen for keeping their real selves protected, opening up only when it feels totally safe. Some Cancer men have difficulty in relating to other men, as masculinity can seem brutal, aggressive and violent. Others, like the writer Ernest Hemingway, go out of their way to create a macho image, while underneath that boozy, big-game hunting, hard-man exterior lies a vulnerable and sensitive human being.

Mother and Child

Mother looms large in the life of all Cancerians. Depending on your childhood, you'll love her or loathe her, be close to her or want to keep her at the end of a long, forked stick. If she's wounded you deeply, you may try to exclude her from your life, either physically or emotionally, but what she represents doesn't go away that easily. Your challenge is to build a healthy support system for yourself instead of blaming others for not providing your bliss.

This means taking responsibility for creating a safe comfort zone to come back to from your excursions into the outside world. You do love to roam, but north, south, east or west, home, for you, is always best. Psychologically, it is vital for you to have a base, even if it's just one that's in your head. It's also vital for you to get out and about, otherwise you'll become increasingly timid and reclusive and your world will shrink to the size of your own four walls. You hate discomfort, either mental or physical, and have a wonderful knack of creating a warm, loving home, though you are not necessarily domesticated. Many Cancerian homes look like over-stuffed junk shops; it's the atmosphere and warmth of welcome that counts.

Conflicting Emotions

You are a mass of contradictions, moving between anxiety and audacity, timidity and temerity, boldness and bashfulness, activity and apathy, sympathy and selfishness and rashness and reserve. It's all part of your cycle and the creative tension between your need for both security and an independent life. Part of you longs to retreat into the arms of an all-embracing mother figure, to lock all the doors and never, ever leave the safety and comfort of the family fireside. Another part feels the call to make your own way in the world and bring home the bacon.

Indirect Approach

Almost nothing will bring you to open confrontation except the fact or threat of emotional loss, and then you are formidable. Like a crab, you rarely approach what you're after directly. You go at it sideways, looking at something else to distract predators. (Some people with Cancer strong in their charts even walk sideways, drifting towards their companions and unintentionally bumping them into walls and off pavements.) Once you have made up your mind that you want something, nothing will persuade you to give up until you have it. You won't be aggressive or even obvious, though you may not be able to resist the odd nip or two if the competition is getting too threatening. Once what you want is in your possession, you'll never let it go. Being a master or mistress of passive resistance, you just hold it tightly in your pincer-like grip and simply refuse to budge.

Keeping Cancer Healthy

Being so sensitive to your environment, your body responds powerfully to changes of climates and seasons, often making you listless at the autumn and spring equinoxes, around the times the clocks change. If this happens, allow yourself some quiet time to let your body catch up with its change of gear. In winter you can go into semi-hibernation. Your body might appreciate occasionally going to bed and snuggling down as the light fades, even if it is only five o'clock in the afternoon. Although seeming indulgent, this could help you cope better with winter blues.

Cancer rules the breasts, which nurture new life; the ribcage, which protects the vital organs of heart, lungs and liver; and the stomach, which receives and holds nourishment. It is also associated with the mucous membranes, the moist layers of tissue protecting the body's inner surfaces. If you feel isolated or rejected, problems could crop up in these parts of the body. Other areas that can be affected are the knees and skin, kidneys and bladder and the head and face.

Your health and vitality depends on your emotional state. Apprehension and anxiety, especially about loved ones or money, can make you ill. Resentment can eat away at you, leading to gall bladder or stomach problems. If you confront what's causing the apprehension, you'll often find it's not so terrible – your avoidance tactics, plus a vivid imagination, can make monsters out of miniscules. Fortunately, you are just as powerfully affected by positive thoughts and emotions, like optimism, cheerfulness and kindliness, which can promote deep healing. Your best medicine can be to flush out negative emotions immediately you spot them, to prevent any toxic build-up.

Cancer at Work

Dynamic Cancerians are often found in prominent positions in large corporations. Cancer women especially can be highly successful in the business world. Quietly ambitious, you enjoy directing others from behind, running your businesses like an extended family, often taking your employees' needs and views into consideration, like entrepreneurial tycoon Richard Branson. Insecurity is what drives you on, and security — both financial and emotional — is your ultimate goal, so the more successful you are, the safer you'll feel.

Supply and Demand

You have a truly uncanny sense of what the public wants and can supply it, making a tidy profit for yourself at the same time. You tend to watch and wait patiently, playing it by instinct and lunging in when you see an opening. Many Cancerians have a natural flair for working in the caring professions, making excellent nurses, nannies, social workers, counsellors and therapists. Teaching, training, and cooking and catering can also appeal.

Money, Money, Money

You're shrewd and responsible with money and drive a hard bargain. It's a rare Cancerian that will take a major risk without having a financial safety net in place in case it fails — so most of your investments and ventures do succeed but over-caution can sometimes hold you back. You may prefer to work with someone else's money, rather than risking your own. Once you sink any capital into an enterprise, you'll watch it like a hawk. Though you're a bit of a skinflint, when people are genuinely in trouble you will help out. When asked for pocket money, my Cancerian grandfather used to dip into his waistcoat pocket, caress a small coin between his fingers for a while before bringing it out reluctantly and handing it over with an audible sigh.

Cancer Relationships

Rather than take emotional risks by allowing anyone to get close, some Cancerians either bypass entanglements altogether or dip in and out of superficial relationships where their feelings can't get hurt. But barricading feelings in doesn't make them go away. Like Sleeping Beauty behind the thorny hedge, they just slumber and can slowly be brought back to life, through time and tenderness, when you meet the right person.

Your life is at its richest with familiar people to respond to. Without relationships of some kind – with family, friends or neighbours, as well as romantic – you're liable to curl up into a tight little ball and play sloth. Because you're so afraid of humiliation and looking ridiculous, you'll rarely approach the object of your affections or interest directly without taking a few precautions to minimise the risk of rejection. When you've set your heart on someone, though, you'll manoeuvre yourself into his or her life and once you've got a foothold, you'll cling on tightly, refusing to let go, or to take no for an answer.

Fair Shares

You love to spoil and pet your partner, and as you love to be needed, you may be attracted to wounded people, then become sullen and seething if you're always pleasing and providing and mopping up after them, without being appreciated. It's tempting then to start to undermine them with subtle criticisms. It may be healthier to borrow some of the qualities of your opposite sign, Capricorn. Think long-term, and realistically, about *your* wants and needs, and whether prospective partners could actually provide a good return on the investment of all the loving attention you'd lavish on them. That may not be very romantic, but it saves disappointment and wasting your precious gifts on those who can't value them.

Exclusively Yours

Being so creative with human raw materials, you may see your partners as projects to be shaped and improved. Many people are perfectly happy the way they are, though, and will resist fiercely any attempts to change them into someone they're not. This can lead to battles and bruised feelings – yours. The more insecure you are in relationships, the more clingy and possessive you become. Because you have an awesome command of atmospheres, you can work subtly on other people's emotions to your own advantage to try to keep your partner by your side. This can be dangerous territory, as it's all too easy to slide into guilt-provoking emotional blackmail. Nobody likes to feel manipulated, so while this strategy may work short-term, eventually the resentment created will bring what you fear most – loss of intimacy. It can be hard to trust that temporary separations do not equal abandonment, but genuine love allows spaces in the togetherness for each of you to develop as separate individuals.

Lust and Marriage

Though some Cancerians undoubtedly do wander, home is usually where you'll come back to, and stay. If a relationship turns sour, you'll just gradually withdraw and find your emotional nurture elsewhere. Divorce is hard for you but, long-suffering as you are, there's a limit to what you'll put up with and betrayal of trust or constant humiliation will eventually tip the balance. As you hate unpleasantness and feeling guilty, you may manipulate the situation to drive your partner out and then get all the sympathy for being left. You're rarely driven by animal passions so bodice-ripping is not your scene, unless some raunchier signs, like Aries or Scorpio, feature large in your chart. Touching and stroking, gentleness and consideration are what turn you on. You're romantic and sentimental and enjoy giving and receiving those tender little tokens that say 'I adore you'. By allowing the natural rhythm of space and intimacy into your relationship, you really can create a marriage made in heaven.

SIX

Aspects of the Sun

PLANETS, JUST LIKE PEOPLE, CAN HAVE IMPORTANT RELATIONSHIPS with each other. These relationships are called aspects. Aspects to your Sun from any other planet can influence your personality markedly. The most powerful effects come with those from the slower-moving planets — Saturn, Uranus, Neptune or Pluto. Sometimes they can alter your ideas about yourself and your behaviour patterns so much that you may not feel at all typical of your sign in certain areas of your life.

Check if your birth date and year appear in the various sections below to find out if one or more of these planets was aspecting the Sun when you were born. Only the so-called challenging aspects have been included. These are formed when the planets are together, opposite or at right angles to each other in the sky.

Unfortunately, because space is restricted, other aspects have been left out, although they have similar effects to those described below and, for the same reason, a few dates will inevitably have been missed out, too. (You can find out for sure whether or not your Sun is aspected at my website www.janeridderpatrick.com) If your Sun has no aspects to Saturn, Uranus, Neptune or Pluto, you're more likely to be a typical Cancer.

Some well-known Cancerians with challenging aspects to their Suns appear below. You can find more in the birthday section at the end of the book.

Sun in Cancer in Aspect with Saturn

If you were born between 1944 and 1946 or 1973 and 1975, whether or not your birthday is listed below, you are likely to feel the influence of Saturn on your Sun.

21 June–1 July in: 1930–7, 1944, 1951–2, 1959, 1966–7, 1974, 1981, 1988–9 and 1996

2–11 July in: 1931, 1938, 1945, 1952–3, 1960, 1967, 1974, 1982, 1989–90 and 1997

12–22 July in: 1931, 1939, 1946, 1953–4, 1961, 1968–9, 1975–6, 1983, 1990 and 1997–8

Pamela Anderson	Barbara Cartland	Edward Heath
Lord Louis Mountbatten	Emmeline Pankhurst	Kenneth Starr

A Sun–Saturn aspect is sometimes referred to as an indicator of a self-made person. Because you can worry, secretly, that you're not quite good enough just the way you are, you're driven to prove yourself to those in authority, by doing, or becoming, whatever you feel will earn you their stamp of approval. This can mean passing all the right exams – or even altering your appearance, like Pamela Anderson. Saturn aspecting your Sun can turn you into a workaholic if you let it. There can be a nagging accuser inside your head spiking your pleasure with discouraging comments about your initiative, appearance, earning power or prospects. This persecutor can also be turned outward, on others. US senator Kenneth Starr was fiercely critical of President Bill Clinton's extramarital affairs and went to extraordinary lengths to expose him.

Yet this same inner critic can become one of your greatest allies if you refuse to take it at face value. Don't let it hold you back by the fear that you might not be up to much or that, if you're judged and found inadequate, you'll be humiliated and even rejected publicly, which is your worst nightmare. It is simply the voice of your powerful ambition to succeed and make something of your life. Most especially, you want to build a secure nest and position for you and yours, and to make a responsible contribution to society. Emmeline Pankhurst put in long hours, tirelessly campaigning for votes for women. Your task is to set your own standards and goals, which may or may not correspond to those of your family or society, and follow this up with a few calculated risks and some disciplined work to achieve them. Then the world is your oyster. You *can* do it. Just remember to stop and enjoy your success – frequently.

Sun in Cancer in Aspect with Uranus

If you were born between 1948 and 1956, whether or not your birthday is listed below, you are likely to feel the influence of Uranus on your Sun.

21 June –1 July in: 1926–30, 1948–52, 1968–72 and 1988–91
2–11 July in: 1928–32, 1951–4, 1971–4 and 1990–94
12–22 July in: 1931–4, 1953–6, 1973–5 and 1992–96

Thomas Barnardo	King Henry VIII	Imelda Marcos
Frida Kahlo	George Sand	Marc Chagall

Shy, timid and retiring or not, no way will you just fall into line with authority because it says you should. In fact, there is part of you that just itches to flout convention. Henry VIII defied the Pope, then the most powerful spiritual authority in the western world, in order to divorce Catherine of Aragon and marry Anne Boleyn in the hope of fathering a son.

A cautious and canny Cancer Sun linked with Uranus, the revolutionary, can be an uneasy mix. You need security, but there's something in you that feels slightly on edge, as though the rug is just about to be pulled from under your feet – or that you're going to yank it away yourself. You're never quite satisfied with the way things, or you yourself, are. If you become too settled and successful, you may be tempted to chuck it all in and do something new, as you thrive on excitement, change and living on the edge. The paintings of the Mexican artist Frida Kahlo, who led a wild, unpredictable life, were once described as 'a ribbon round a bomb'. You may also have the periodic urge to go off abruptly and do your own thing, which conflicts with your intense need for intimacy. It's vitally important to find some way of expressing both of these sides of your nature without either sabotaging home and family or choking with boredom. This combination often works best when you band together with like-minded people in innovative or humanitarian projects, preferably those that would help make the world a better place for those in need of care and protection – Thomas Barnardo, while still a medical student, opened his own Ragged School in London, and then went on to establish homes for destitute children.

Sun in Cancer in Aspect with Neptune

21 June–1 July in: 1942–9 and 1983–9
2–11 July in: 1947–54 and 1988–94
12–22 July in: 1952–8 and 1992–8

Estée Lauder	Marcel Proust	George Orwell
Esther Rantzen	Carly Simon	Prince William

You are powerfully affected by the sufferings of others, especially women and children, and long to alleviate them. Esther Rantzen set up ChildLine, a free telephone helpline for children at risk. Others may have an unrealistic picture of you, as you sometimes do yourself. You could be seen as an ideal – or idol – of perfection, or as a victim, or rescuer – or all three. You may feel helpless, or even flawed in some way, and then become heavily dependent on your father, boss or partner to shore up your confidence.

This can be a winning combination for creative work like writing, acting, painting or advertising because you are a catcher and provider of dreams. You know what magic people yearn for, and are inspired to provide it. Estée Lauder did this with her glamorous perfumes and cosmetics. The caring professions could attract you too, but learning to make firm boundaries is essential, as you tend to take on far too much because you feel over-responsible and guilty if you say no. Finding an ideal to serve, possibly a spiritual one, that you believe in whole-heartedly, can transform your life. Until you do, you could be endlessly longing for a vague 'something' that's disappointingly and tantalisingly just out of reach. Sometimes your openness to life and its pain can be overwhelming and you long to retreat. The French writer Marcel Proust did just that, but found that the only way to heal suffering is to experience it to the full. Frequent holidays from everyday reality are essential, but be careful not to over-use the escape routes of alcohol or food, as addictions and allergies are common with this aspect. Music, meditation or simple daydreaming are far better options.

Sun in Cancer in Aspect with Pluto

Those born between 1913 and 1939, whether or not their birthdays are listed below, are likely to feel the influence of Pluto on their Sun.

21 June–1 July in: 1970–7
2–11 July in: 1923–33 and 1976–82
12–22 July in: 1930–40 and 1979–86

Myra Hindley	Elisabeth Kübler-Ross	Ellen MacArthur
John D. Rockefeller	Donald Rumsfeld	Ken Russell

One thing is certain – you are a force to be reckoned with. Your power is formidable, all the more so because it is rarely upfront and abrasive but radiates out quietly as an indomitable quality of personality. When you set your heart on something, you give it your all. With almost superhuman endurance, tiny yachtswoman Ellen MacArthur has won tough world-class trophies and universal affection. A couple of cautions though: both Cancer and Pluto can be underhand and even cruel when feeling vulnerable. You can play your cards close to your chest about your ambitions for fear of loss or attack if you let slip too much about yourself. Know that with the resources at your disposal, you are more than adequately armed for anything that life could ever throw at you.

Motivation is all with this aspect. What you give out, you'll get back, with interest, whether that is good or evil.

You are a survivor and are likely to go through several major life-changes that will transform you. Pluto aspects usually bring an interest in power, sex, secrets, death and wealth and it would be surprising if your career, or that of your partner, did not involve one or more of these. Two extreme examples on the same theme are Myra Hindley and Elisabeth Kübler-Ross, whose lives were bound up with death. Hindley, as a murderer, was an agent of death, while Kübler-Ross investigated the stages of dying and helped countless terminally ill people, and their relatives, to reconcile themselves to the inevitable end of life. Like billionaire industrialist and philanthropist, John D. Rockefeller, power and money may be more your territory and with your sensitive antennae for what others need and you ability to provide it, you can be remarkably shrewd and successful in both business and political affairs.

SEVEN

Meeting Your Moon

☽ THE GLYPH FOR THE MOON IS THE SEMI-CIRCLE OR CRESCENT. It is a symbol for the receptiveness of the soul and is associated with feminine energies and the ebb and flow of the rhythms of life. In some Islamic traditions it represents the gateway to paradise and the realms of bliss.

The Sun and Moon are the two complementary poles of your personality, like yang and yin, masculine and feminine, active and reflective, career and home, father and mother. The Moon comes into its own as a guide at night, the time of sleeping consciousness. It also has a powerful effect on the waters of the earth. Likewise, the Moon in your birth chart describes what you respond to instinctively and feel 'in your waters', often just below the level of consciousness. It is your private radar system, sending you messages via your body responses and feelings, telling you whether a situation seems safe or scary, nice or nasty. Feelings provide vital information about circumstances in and around you. Ignore them at your peril; that will lead you into emotional, and sometimes even physical, danger. Eating disorders tend to be associated with being out of touch with, or neglecting, the instincts and the body, both of which the Moon describes.

Extraordinary though it might seem to those who are emotionally tuned in, some people have great difficulty in knowing what they are feeling. One simple way is to pay attention to your body. Notice any sensations that attract your attention. Those are linked to your feelings. Now get a sense of whether they are pleasant or unpleasant, then try to put a more exact name to what those feelings might be. Is it sadness, happiness, fear? What is it that they are trying to tell you? Your Moon hints at what will strongly activate your feelings. Learning to trust and decode this information will help make the world seem — and be — a safer place.

The Moon represents your drive to nurture and protect yourself and others. Its sign, house and aspects describe how you respond and adapt emotionally to situations and what feeds you, in every sense of the word. It gives information about your home and home life and how you experienced your mother, family and childhood, as well as describing your comfort zone of what feels familiar — the words 'family' and 'familiar' come from the same source. It shows, too, what makes you feel secure and what could comfort you when you're feeling anxious. Your Moon describes what moves and motivates you powerfully at the deepest instinctual level and indicates what is truly the 'matter' in — or with — your life.

Knowing children's Moon signs can help parents and teachers better understand their insecurities and respect their emotional make-up and needs, and so prevent unnecessary hurt, or even harm, to sensitive young lives. It's all too easy to expect that our children and parents should have the same emotional wiring as we do, but that's rarely how life works. Finding our parents' Moon signs can be a real revelation. It can often help us understand where they are coming from, what they need and why they react to us in the way they do. Many of my clients have been able to find the understanding and compassion to forgive their parents when they realised that they were doing their very best with the emotional resources available to them.

In relationships it is important that your Moon's requirements are met to a good enough extent. For example, if you have your Moon in Sagittarius you must have adventure, freedom and the opportunity to express your beliefs. If being with your partner constantly violates these basic needs, you will never feel secure and loved and the relationship could, in the long term, undermine you. However, if your Moon feels too comfortable, you will never change and grow. The art is to get a good working balance between support and challenge.

A man's Moon sign can show some of the qualities he will unconsciously select in a wife or partner. Some of the others are shown in his Venus sign. Many women can seem much more like their Moon signs than their Sun signs, especially if they are involved in mothering a family and being a support system for their husbands or partners. It is only at the mid-life crisis that many women start to identify more with the qualities of their own Suns rather than living that out through their partners' ambitions. Similarly, men tend to live out the characteristics of their Moon signs through their wives and partners until mid-life, often quite cut off from their own feelings and emotional responses. If a man doesn't seem at all like his Moon sign, then check out the women in his life. There's a good chance that his wife, mother or daughter will show these qualities.

Your Moon can be in any sign, including the same one as your Sun. Each sign belongs to one of the four elements: Fire, Earth, Air or Water. The element of your Moon can give you a general idea of how you respond to new situations and what you need to feel safe and comforted. We all become anxious if our Moon's needs are not being recognised and attended to. We then, automatically, go into our personal little rituals for making ourselves feel better. Whenever you are feeling distressed, especially when you are way out of your comfort zone in an unfamiliar situation, do something to feed and soothe your Moon. You're almost certain to calm down quickly.

Fire Moons

If you have a fire Moon in Aries, Leo or Sagittarius, your first response to any situation is to investigate in your imagination the possibilities for drama, excitement and self-expression. Feeling trapped by dreary routine in an ordinary humdrum life crushes you completely. Knowing that you are carrying out a special mission feeds your soul. To you, all the world's a stage and a voyage of discovery. Unless you are at the centre of the action playing some meaningful role, anxiety and depression can set in. To feel secure, you have to have an appropriate outlet for expressing your spontaneity, honourable instincts and passionate need to be of unique significance. The acknowledgement, appreciation and feedback of people around you are essential, or you don't feel real. Not to be seen and appreciated, or to be overlooked, can feel like a threat to your very existence.

Earth Moons

If you have an earth Moon in Taurus, Virgo or Capricorn, you'll respond to new situations cautiously and practically. Rapidly changing circumstances where you feel swept along and out of control are hard for you to cope with. You need time for impressions to sink in. Sometimes it is only much later, after an event has taken place, that you become sure what you felt about it. Your security lies in slowing down, following familiar routines and rituals, even if they are a bit obsessive, and focusing on something, preferably material – possibly the body itself or nature – which is comforting because it is still there. Indulging the senses in some way often helps too, through food, sex, or body care. So does taking charge of the practicalities of the immediate situation, even if this is only mixing the drinks or passing out clipboards. To feel secure, you need continuity and a sense that you have your hand on the rudder of your own life. Think of the rather irreverent joke about the man seeming to cross himself in a crisis, all the while actually touching his most valued possessions to check that they are still intact – spectacles, testicles, wallet and watch. That must have been thought up by someone with the Moon in an earth sign.

Air Moons

When your Moon is in an air sign – Gemini, Libra or Aquarius – you feel most secure when you can stand back from situations and observe them from a distance. Too much intimacy chokes you and you'll tend to escape it by going into your head to the safety of ideas and analysis. Even in close relationships you need your mental, and preferably physical, space. You often have to think, talk or write about what you are feeling before you are sure what your feelings are. By putting them 'out there' so that you can examine them clearly, you can claim them as your own. Unfairness and unethical behaviour can upset you badly and make you feel uneasy until you have done something about it or responded in some way. It can be easy with an air Moon to be unaware of, or to ignore, your own feelings because you are more responsive to ideas, people and situations outside of yourself that may seem to have little connection with you. This is not a good idea, as it cuts you off from the needs of your body as well as your own emotional intelligence. Making opportunities to talk, play with and exchange ideas and information can reduce the stress levels if anxiety strikes.

Water Moons

Finally, if your Moon is in a water sign — Cancer, Scorpio or Pisces — you are ultra-sensitive to atmospheres, and you can experience other people's pain or distress as if they were your own. You tend to take everything personally and, even if the situation has nothing at all to do with you, feel responsible for making it better. Your worst nightmare is to feel no emotional response coming back from other people. That activates your deep-seated terror of abandonment, which can make you feel that you don't exist and is, quite literally, what you fear even more than death. If you feel insecure, you may be tempted to resort to emotional manipulation to try to force intimacy with others — not a good idea, as this can lead to the very rejection that you dread. You are at your most secure when the emotional climate is positive and you have trusted, supportive folk around who will winkle you out of hiding if you become too reclusive. With a water Moon, it is vital to learn to value your own feelings and to take them seriously — and to have a safe, private place you can retreat to when you feel emotionally fragile. As you never forget anything which has made a feeling impression on you, sometimes your reactions are triggered by unconscious memories of things long past, rather than what is taking place in the present. When you learn to interpret them correctly, your feelings are your finest ally and will serve you well.

Finding Your Moon Sign

If you don't yet know your Moon sign, before looking it up, you could have some fun reading through the descriptions that follow and seeing if you can guess which one it is. To find your Moon sign, check your year and date of birth in the tables on pp. 99–112. For a greater in-depth understanding of your Moon sign, you might like to read about its characteristics in the book in this series about that sign.

At the beginning of each section are the names of some well-known Cancerians with that particular Moon sign. You can find more about them in Chapter Ten.

Sun in Cancer with Moon in Aries

Pamela Anderson	Barbara Cartland	King Henry VIII
Sir Edmund Hillary	Diana Rigg	George Sand

Action and drama and plenty of it will come your way — either in real life or in your work. Think of Pamela Anderson as a lifeguard in *Baywatch*, and Diana Rigg's action-woman role as Emma Peel in *The Avengers*. Whatever you do, you'll plunge into it with energy and gusto. Impulsive and daring, you live for the moment and often fail to reflect on the consequences of rash words and actions until they have been said and done. You'll follow your own romantic ideals whatever the cost. Novelist George Sand left her husband and children for a bohemian life in 1831 and had a string of lovers, including the composer Chopin. An Aries Moon can exaggerate the boldness–bashfulness seesaw of your Cancer Sun. In action mode, you can be so focused on pushing through your own affairs that you can seem bossy and less than sensitive to others' needs and interests. Then, when people around hit back, you'll curl up into a tight little prickly ball, depressed and anxious that people don't like you because you've offended them.

You don't, however, need to cling to the offensive, offending and offended cycle. You can put all that dynamic energy into creative projects and adventures or into competing in business. When you're below par, throwing yourself into heavy housework or renovation can have you feeling better in no time. Once you have mastered the art of sticking up for yourself without either fearfulness or force, you will have cracked the code for contentment with this combination. Getting your teeth into a challenge too, the tougher the better, makes you feel secure. Like Sir Edmund Hillary, who, with Tenzing Norgay, was the first to reach the summit of the world's highest mountain, you are at your best when you find, and set about tackling, your own personal Mount Everest.

Sun in Cancer with Moon in Taurus

| Frida Kahlo | Imelda Marcos | Marcel Proust |
| Terence Stamp | Meryl Streep | Natalie Wood |

As material security is of the utmost importance to you, if your bank balance sinks below a certain level you will start to feel jittery. Fortunately, you are well-equipped with the ways, means and determination to make sure that the wolf stays well away from your door. It would be surprising if you haven't created a welcoming nest that you own, filled with beauty, tranquillity and comfort. Peace, routine, sensuality and stability, especially on the home front, are also important. Woe betide anyone who tries to take that from you! Unless you have other, wilder, patterns in your birth chart, you hate to be jolted out of your accustomed routine too abruptly and you'll go to great lengths to ensure that all runs smoothly and undisturbed – and under your control. Though some with this Moon, because sex is such a comfort, may stray a little, at heart you prefer to stay true, as disruption is something you don't risk lightly. Even if things are tough, what's known and familiar is best. Both actress Natalie Wood and artist Frida Kahlo remarried men they'd divorced.

Sharing food, glorious food and memories of the past will always be of interest. Marcel Proust began his major work, *In Search of Lost Time*, describing having tea with his mother and eating little shell-shaped cakes called madeleines. It was their scent, as he dipped them into his lime-blossom tea in adulthood, that transported him back to his long-forgotten days of childhood – and 13 volumes of rich introspection followed. More prosaically, actor Terence Stamp has marketed gluten-free bread, baked to his own specifications. With a wheat intolerance, he found it hard to get interesting, yet safe, foodstuffs, and wanted to help others in the same position to be able to enjoy eating without discomfort.

Sun in Cancer with Moon in Gemini

Julie Burchill	Trevor Eve	Lord Louis Mountbatten
Franz Kafka	Dianne Feinstein	Nathaniel Hawthorne

With your lively mind and quick wit, you stand out from other Cancerians who usually prefer to withdraw and sulk if they feel insecure, rather than, like you, throw a sharp verbal dart back at the source of their troubles. Sometimes you're oblivious to your feelings until you've stopped for a while to think about what they are, so you can have sudden unexpected outbursts of emotion – then wonder what on earth brought them on. You may even have the impression that two different people live inside you: one sensitive, moody and tender and the other clever, detached and trendy. Your challenge is to keep in touch with the world and all its changing faces, yet stay aware of your own truths too. By flipping your attention backwards and forwards between what's outside you and what's within, you can track both, neither getting trapped in introspective brooding nor being pulled here and there emotionally, at the mercy of every passing whim. Nathaniel Hawthorne and Franz Kafka both chose to write in seclusion and were geniuses at conveying subtleties. With a little practise, you too can communicate feelings brilliantly.

It's hard for you to stick to just one career, or, if you do, to stay in the same position or place too long – and why should you? You need frequent variety and stimulation to keep your mind fed and whirring with fresh ideas and you are probably a skilled negotiator and broker of deals. While travelling refreshes you, another part wants to stay firmly rooted at home so you may prefer to keep a welcoming open house for friends and passing acquaintances, so that the world can come to you.

Sun in Cancer with Moon in Cancer

Anita Brookner	Harrison Ford	Camilla Parker Bowles
George Orwell	Henry David Thoreau	Prince William

Those you consider family – blood relatives or chosen and cherished friends – are at the centre of your world. To feel secure, you need warm, intimate relationships in which you feel totally accepted and where there is plenty of tenderness given and received. Close connections, once established, are likely to last forever. Often quite reclusive, you need to retreat when overwhelmed by too much human contact. You probably have, or dream of having, a little bolthole in the country where you can create a cosy world of your own and play happy families. You like to build protective barriers between you and 'them' out there, to pull up the drawbridge and relax and be informal with your own folks. Harrison Ford loves to get away with his family to their remote farmhouse; and American poet Thoreau, the 'hermit of Walden', spent months alone in the woods away from civilisation, living in harmony with nature.

With your intense sensitivity to atmospheres and fear of abandonment, if your childhood was insecure or troubled, to cope with your fears and pain you could have erected almost impenetrable defences and behaviour patterns, which you'll cling to tenaciously. But, as the saying goes, it's never too late to have a happy childhood. What is important is that you learn to build up warm supportive relationships with those who can be trusted, and firmly exclude those who can't. Man or woman, you have a powerful instinct to mother, and be mothered. Curled up in a protective cocoon, well away from dangers, physical and emotional, is where you want to be and, unless you have been terribly rejected and damaged in childhood, you'll be equally loving and protective of nature and anything or anyone you see as vulnerable.

Sun in Cancer with Moon in Leo

P.T. Barnum	Rodolfo Gucci	Tom Hanks
Estée Lauder	George Michael	Nancy Reagan

Somewhere, somehow, you have got to find a place in the limelight, preferably solo. At heart you're a star, possibly even a bit of a prima donna, and can enjoy dressing beautifully. This can be an enormously creative combination, giving a love of drama, glamour and the arts. You've got the confidence to strut your stuff, plus the sensitivity to know what an audience wants, and the ability to deliver the goods. Provided you learn to cope with the normal frustrations, setbacks and humiliating egg on the face that almost inevitably come with creating and performing, you can go far. You may have a fascination with what's sensational in human nature and can feel great empathy and protectiveness towards those who are excluded for being different, stepping in to help where you can. P.T. Barnum was a flamboyant American showman who created the 'greatest show on earth' and made a fortune through sponsoring those who were then, unkindly, called 'freaks'.

You need recognition and prestige and, though you can be tender and touchingly loyal, you can also be fiercely proud and sometimes a little vain. Love them or hate them, family does matter, and you could have a bit of a struggle to square up your instinctive need to play a central role with your equally pressing desire to belong to your clan. Rodolfo Gucci, one of the founders of the family saddler's business which turned into a luxurious fashion empire, came to blows with his brother in the boardroom; and when more family members joined the team, it degenerated into a full-on family feud. You thrive when you are at the head of your own family, biological or chosen, dispensing wisdom, direction and loving, benevolent dictatorship.

Sun in Cancer with Moon in Virgo

John Bradshaw   Richard Branson   Judy Chicago
The Dalai Lama   Gregor Mendel   Emmeline Pankhurst

Tea and sympathy are all well and good as far as you are concerned, but you feel the need to go further and engage in hands-on activity that produces concrete results. Whatever you do, you like to do well and can't bear incompetence or shoddy workmanship. Usually a Virgo Moon knows when to say no, but as you like to see a job through you can end up working all hours. Take care not to become a workaholic and miss out on the rewards of all that labour.

You are at your happiest when you have a task to carry out and are being of practical service. For some, this is a life mission, like the Dalai Lama, who feeds the spiritual and emotional needs of the world, as well as of his native land, Tibet. Father Gregor Mendel spent years in his monastery garden crossbreeding peas, patiently and painstakingly noting the characteristics of each plant, from generation to generation, and then analysing the results. Though it wasn't appreciated in his lifetime, he is now recognised as the father of modern genetics. Others, like Richard Branson, prefer to take on shorter-term tasks at frequent intervals, with faster results and more variety. It's interesting that Branson has named his company Virgin. Perhaps he knows his astrology.

On a bad day, you can be hypersensitive and anxious,

and even crabby and critical. If that happens, put your house in order, literally. There is nothing like straightening your pencils and colour-coding your notebooks to make the world feel a better place. You can be excellent in business, combining Cancer canniness with Virgo realism and the willingness to tackle any job that needs to be done with matter-of-fact humility.

Sun in Cancer with Moon in Libra

Isabelle Adjani	Arthur Ashe	George W. Bush
Antoni Gaudí	Käthe Kollwitz	Donald Rumsfeld

Libra is the sign of the designer. Sometimes this is literal, as in the case of Spain's finest architect Antoni Gaudí, creator of the magnificent Church of the Holy Family in Barcelona. Your designs, however, may be to create the right conditions to ensure security and plenty for you and yours, as are the tasks of US President George W. Bush and his defence secretary, Donald Rumsfeld,

Many people with Libra Moons feel more at home with the opposite sex, rather than their own. With your natural charm and relaxed manner, you know how to make people feel welcome and at their ease. You hate direct confrontation and like to be – or be seen as – Ms or Mr Nice. Taken too far, in your bid to be fair and to please, you can end up being far too altruistic and letting other people make your decisions for you. The pendulum, however, can also swing the other way and sometimes you may become touchy about how unfair life is to you, or to those you identify with. You may appear to be a meek and mild pushover but anybody who underestimates you is in for a few surprises. Behind that gentle manner is the mind of a general and the tenacity of a terrier. You have your opponents sized up and know where they are coming from and what they want. You'll bide your time and, when the circumstances are right, you'll pounce. Your major challenges are to learn to trust your own judgement, identify your own principles and to stand up for them. Once you have done that, you are formidable at getting your own way, with everyone thinking that it was their idea in the first place.

Sun in Cancer with Moon in Scorpio

Roald Amundsen	John Cusack	Myra Hindley
Nelson Mandela	Mary Wesley	Colin Wilson

It has been said that when Scorpio is good, it is not simply good, it's saintly – but when it is bad it's evil. This is a bit of an exaggeration. Most don't go to the extremes of Myra Hindley, the vicious child-murderer, or Nelson Mandela, who endured 29 years of imprisonment, then walked out with his integrity and vision undented and went on to be the first, and highly respected, black South African president. You are likely to have an interest in poking deeply into those places and subjects that normal, nice people tend to approach more moderately – like sex, corruption, power and the dark mysteries of life, death and the occult. You can make a first-class researcher or, like novelist Mary Wesley, a sensitive observer of life's darker side.

You have access to immense emotional power that you can turn to making money, influencing political decisions and exposing and eliminating corruption – or just manipulating others to do what you want. Underneath that reserved exterior bubbles a cauldron of passion, and possibly intrigue. You can take slights personally where none was intended and plot revenge for years. Remember Mandela, and know that the best revenge is a noble-hearted modesty that shrinks enemies down to size. You can be highly sensual, and sex is therapeutic for you. Without it, or a substitute — like facing intense challenges or power-brokering — you can become irritable and moody. It is only too easy to allow yourself to sink into a swamp of resentment and black depression where your feelings overwhelm you. You are astute in business, as you are highly intuitive and can work well with people if you can keep your tetchiness and touchiness under control.

Sun in Cancer with Moon in Sagittarius

Wendy Cope	Gerald Ford	Ellen MacArthur
Paul Merton	Mervyn Peake	John Wesley

Outgoing and exuberant, your Moon in Sagittarius can encourage your more timid Cancer Sun to trust life and have faith in the future. Sometimes this optimism can get the better of you, for when you're in your stride you're apt to believe you can walk through walls, break all the rules — and get away with it. You can be a bit of a gambler and wild child, dicing with life or luck or love, because of your sense of being divinely protected. And possibly you are — Sagittarius is the sign associated with lucky escapes. In 1975 US President Gerald Ford escaped unharmed from two assassination attempts by two different people in the same month, while plucky yachtswoman Ellen MacArthur seems to relish death-defying drama on the high seas. You probably love to travel, either physically or in your imagination, constantly pushing back the boundaries of your experience and getting out and about to meet new people and explore new places.

Being a natural philosopher, you're on a life-long quest to find and understand the meaning of life. When you've found a fresh nugget of wisdom, you love to pass it on. You make an inspiring and entertaining teacher or preacher and a warm and inspiring guide to those under your care, though you may have to watch a tendency to moralising. Restraint and doing things on a small scale has minimal appeal. John Wesley, the evangelist who founded Methodism, during his 50 years of ministry in the eighteenth century travelled 250,000 miles, preached over 40,000 sermons and frequently crowds of between 10,000 and 30,000 people would wait patiently for hours to hear him. 'I look on the whole world as my parish,' he said, and so do you.

Sun in Cancer with Moon in Capricorn

Ambrose Bierce	Edgar Degas	John Dee
Ernest Hemingway	Sue Lawley	Liv Tyler

Highly ambitious to earn recognition and to prove yourself, you are tenacious in reaching the goals you crave — status, success and respect. Hard work and taking on responsibility are as familiar to you as breathing. John Dee was a gifted mathematician and geographer who came to high office as Queen Elizabeth I's adviser, spy and astrologer. As a young man, he used to study for eighteen hours a day. Many with this combination have come from poor or humble backgrounds and work their way steadily to the top or were raised in homes where correct behaviour and discipline were the rule, depriving you of warm acceptance for simply being you. There's a bonus in this: you are well able to look after yourself and, unless you give in to the periodic black patches of hopelessness that can dog you, you're headed up the ladder of success, rung by careful rung. The American writer Hemingway chose to shoot himself because of his deep depressions (though his heavy drinking was doubtless a contributory factor). Sometimes deliberately allowing yourself to feel melancholy, instead of fighting it, may help it lift more quickly.

You've a wry sense of the ridiculous that may verge on the cynical. Ambrose Bierce's *Devil's Dictionary* is a classic of black humour. He defines a saint, for example, as 'a dead sinner revised and edited'. This is a useful combination for creating success in the media and in business, as you're a realist with your finger on the pulse of what the public needs. You make a loyal and responsible partner, and if you can work out a way of balancing your home life with your ambitions, you can have the best of both worlds. Don't forget to enjoy them.

Sun in Cancer with Moon in Aquarius

Diahann Carroll	Marc Chagall	Princess Diana
Mary Baker Eddy	Iris Murdoch	Cat Stevens

Cancer needs endless reassurance and loving acceptance, while Aquarius can be as detached and aloof as a scientist. This combination can make you appear contrary, even to yourself, as you swing from desire for intimacy and closeness to cutting off brusquely because of an overwhelming need for space. Emotionally, you live with the anxiety that your security could be shattered at any moment so it's hard for you to relax. You could, like Princess Diana, have a difficult relationship with your body, especially if you focus more on helping others than paying attention to your own physical and emotional needs. History and traditions can fascinate you, yet you loathe being expected to take part, year after year, in what you consider senseless, outworn rituals. You are a rebel and a mould-breaker, with a strong sense of family.

You may often feel like an alien or outsider, hovering on the edge, like a beggar child with its nose pressed against the baker's window, smelling the delicious food which is tantalisingly out of reach. Your home or your work could be odd or experimental. Chagall painted, in extraordinary colours, a strange jumble of animals, objects and people from his dreams, past life and from Russian folklore. You have the gift of friendship, and identify strongly with outsiders and those who are excluded. Working in teams of like-minded people gives you great satisfaction, especially in humanitarian or ethical projects aimed at improving social conditions. Your emotional roots can't be confined to one small pot so you are usually happiest when you can expand your idea of family to include the world at large, and may even enjoy living in a community or having your doors wide open for those who are just passing through.

Sun in Cancer with Moon in Pisces

Kathy Bates	Hermann Hesse	Gustav Klimt
Ginger Rogers	Robin Williams	The Duke of Windsor

Being so sensitive and suggestible, you need to take responsibility for choosing carefully those you allow into your intimate circle – or even associate with frequently. It's all too easy for you to be sucked into other people's realities and be used, or manipulated, by stronger personalities through guilt or seduction. You may prefer to retreat into your imagination or out of the action, rather than confront harsh realities. Hermann Hesse's *The Glass Bead Game* is a Utopian fantasy of withdrawal from the world. Pisces chaos together with Cancer clutter often equals a comfortable and lived-in, but rather messy, home life, physically or emotionally.

As you are so easily bruised yourself and can identify with the victim, you hate to see people or animals suffer but you need to guard against becoming a complete pushover for hard-luck stories. Men with this combination may feel threatened by their tender feelings and try to suppress them firmly, and so can appear cynical. You are deeply romantic, yearning for seamless bliss, rather like that depicted in Gustav Klimt's painting *The Kiss*, where two lovers seem to fuse together in an ecstatic embrace.

Occasionally, you may be tempted to use your gift for working atmospheres to misguide others, or to get caught up in fantasising yourself, like Kathy Bates' character in *Misery*, who insinuated herself into a man's life with destructive consequences. The positive side of your sensitivity is that you are equally open to being uplifted and healed by the enchantment of beauty, goodness and love – and passing that on to others too. Your gift of tapping into thoughts and feelings in general circulation and giving them expression is a great blessing, especially if you are a writer, performer or artist.

EIGHT

Mercury – It's All in the Mind

☿ THE GLYPHS FOR THE PLANETS ARE MADE UP OF THREE SYMBOLS: the circle, the semi-circle and the cross. Mercury is the only planet, apart from Pluto, whose glyph is made up of all three of these symbols. At the bottom there is the cross, representing the material world; at the top is the semi-circle of the crescent Moon, symbolising the personal soul; and in the middle, linking these two, is the circle of eternity, expressed through the individual. In mythology, Mercury was the only god who had access to all three worlds – the underworld, the middle world of earth and the higher world of the gods. Mercury in your chart represents your ability, through your thoughts and words, to make connections between the inner world of your mind and emotions, the outer world of other people and events, and the higher world of intuition. Your Mercury sign can give you a great deal of information about the way your mind works and about your interests, communication skills and your preferred learning style.

It can be frustrating when we just can't get through to some people and it's easy to dismiss them as being either completely thick or deliberately obstructive. Chances are they are neither. It may be that you're simply not talking each other's languages. Knowing your own and other people's communication styles can lead to major breakthroughs in relationships.

Information about children's natural learning patterns can help us teach them more effectively. It's impossible to learn properly if the material isn't presented in a way that resonates with the way your mind works. You just can't 'hear' it, pick it up or grasp it. Wires then get crossed and the data simply isn't processed. Many children are seriously disadvantaged if learning materials and environments don't speak to them. You may even have been a child like that yourself. If so, you could easily have been left with the false impression that you are a poor learner just because you couldn't get a handle on the lessons being taught. Identifying your own learning style can be like finding the hidden key to the treasure room of knowledge.

The signs of the zodiac are divided into four groups by element:

> The fire signs: Aries, Leo and Sagittarius
> The earth signs: Taurus, Virgo and Capricorn
> The air signs: Gemini, Libra and Aquarius
> The water signs: Cancer, Scorpio and Pisces

Your Mercury will therefore belong to one of the four elements, depending on which sign it is in. Your Mercury can only be in one of three signs – the same sign as your Sun, the one before or the one after. This means that each sign has one learning style that is never natural to it. For Cancer, this is the earth style.

Mercury in each of the elements has a distinctive way of

operating, I've given the following names to the learning and communicating styles of Mercury through the elements. Mercury in fire – active imaginative; Mercury in earth – practical; Mercury in air – logical; and Mercury in water – impressionable.

Mercury in Fire: Active Imaginative

Your mind is wide open to the excitement of fresh ideas. It responds to action and to the creative possibilities of new situations. Drama, games and storytelling are excellent ways for you to learn. You love to have fun and play with ideas. Any material to be learned has to have some significance for you personally, or add to your self-esteem, otherwise you rapidly lose interest. You learn by acting out the new information, either physically or in your imagination. The most efficient way of succeeding in any goal is to make first a mental picture of your having achieved it. This is called mental rehearsal and is used by many top sportsmen and women as a technique to help improve their performance. You do this spontaneously, as your imagination is your greatest mental asset. You can run through future scenarios in your mind's eye and see, instantly, where a particular piece of information or situation could lead and spot possibilities that other people couldn't even begin to dream of. You are brilliant at coming up with flashes of inspiration for creative breakthroughs and crisis management.

Mercury in Earth: Practical

Endless presentations of feelings, theories and possibilities can make your eyes glaze over and your brain ache to shut down. What really turns you on is trying out these theories and possibilities to see if they work in practice. If they don't, you'll tend to classify them 'of no further interest'. Emotionally charged information is at best a puzzling non-starter and at worst an irritating turn-off. Practical demonstrations, tried and tested facts and working models fascinate you. Hands-on learning, where you can see how a process functions from start to finish, especially if it leads to some useful material end-product, is right up your street. It's important to allow yourself plenty of time when you are learning, writing or thinking out what to say, otherwise you can feel rushed and out of control, never pleasant sensations for earth signs. Your special skill is in coming up with effective solutions to practical problems and in formulating long-range plans that bring concrete, measurable results.

Mercury in Air: Logical
You love learning about, and playing with, ideas, theories and principles. Often you do this best by arguing or bouncing ideas off other people, or by writing down your thoughts. Your special gift is in your ability to stand back and work out the patterns of relationship between people or things. You much prefer it when facts are presented to you logically and unemotionally and have very little time for the irrational, uncertainty or for personal opinions. You do, though, tend to have plenty of those kinds of views yourself, only you call them logical conclusions. Whether a fact is useful or not is less important than whether it fits into your mental map of how the world operates. If facts don't fit in, you'll either ignore them, find a way of making them fit, or, occasionally, make a grand leap to a new, upgraded theory. Yours is the mind of the scientist or chess player. You make a brilliant planner because you can be detached enough to take an overview of the entire situation.

Mercury in Water: Impressionable

Your mind is sensitive to atmospheres and emotional undertones and to the context in which information is presented. Plain facts and figures can often leave you cold and even intimidated. You can take things too personally and read between the lines for what you believe is really being said or taught. If you don't feel emotionally safe, you can be cautious about revealing your true thoughts. It may be hard, or even impossible, for you to learn properly in what you sense is a hostile environment. You are excellent at impression management. Like a skilful artist painting a picture, you can influence others to think what you'd like them to by using suggestive gestures or pauses and intonations. People with Mercury in water signs are often seriously disadvantaged by left-brain schooling methods that are too rigidly structured for them. You take in information best through pictures or images, so that you get a 'feel' for the material and can make an emotional bond with it, in the same way you connect with people. In emotionally supportive situations where there is a rapport between you and your instructors, or your learning material, you are able just to drink in and absorb circulating knowledge without conscious effort, sometimes not even being clear about how or why you know certain things.

Finding Your Mercury Sign

If you don't yet know your Mercury sign, you might like to see if you can guess what it is from the descriptions below before checking it out in the tables on pp. 113–15.

Sun in Cancer with Mercury in Gemini

Olivia de Havilland Nathaniel Hawthorne The Dalai Lama
George Orwell   Lord Kitchener   Prince William

Both Mercury in Gemini and Sun in Cancer are tuned in to what's currently circulating – 'in the air' and in the emotional atmosphere. Combining intuitive feeling with skilful communication is no mean feat. You have the potential of tapping into your own and other people's feelings to identify what is really going on under the surface of the sea of sensations that washes around and through you – and saying it how it is. Writers with this combination are gifted at describing the passion and pathos of relationship tangles, especially those in families.

You are quick to notice fresh trends, often before everyone else, and love to pass on the news. Your head is likely to be well-stocked with curious facts and odd, seemingly useless, pieces of information, folk wisdom and family history that you can produce at exactly the right moment, like a magician pulling a rabbit out of a hat. You'll enjoy getting out and about, meeting new people and keeping up-to-date. Public figures with this mix are often skilled at dealing with the press. Like Lord Kitchener, you can often get people to do exactly what you want with a mixture of clever persuasion and emotionalism. He ran a hugely successful army recruiting campaign with posters showing him pointing directly at the viewer, declaring 'Your country needs you!' This is a wonderful combination for using thoughts and words to make appeals that hit home both emotionally and intellectually about injustice to the vulnerable. The Dalai Lama travels round the world, spreading practical loving kindness as an ambassador for his own troubled country, Tibet, and for universal peace. You have the ability too to heal your world with words.

Sun in Cancer with Mercury in Cancer

Barbara Cartland	Princess Diana	Harrison Ford
Tom Hanks	Emmeline Pankhurst	Richard Wilson

Your mind is acutely sensitive to emotional undercurrents and your focus is less on what people are saying than on the feelings that are being conveyed. Often, after an interchange, you may not be able to remember the exact words that were spoken, but the emotional atmosphere will have left an indelible impression. You certainly won't forget a rejection or putdown, as you are prone to brood, and sometimes can't resist retaliating with a cutting retort. You tend to be touchy and take things personally, which can sometimes cloud your judgement. Some of your ideas may have come, undigested, from family and friends or the popular press. It is useful to check out occasionally whether the opinions you air are genuinely your own, or whether you're just being grumpy like Richard Wilson's character, Victor Meldrew, in *One Foot in the Grave*. Sometimes you may be tempted to say what you think people want to hear, rather than what you really feel or believe. In the art of emotional appeals, you're hard to beat. When Princess Diana was interviewed on television about her private life, she won the hearts of many; others, though, dismissed her as being simply manipulative.

You absorb information best if you have a comfortable and safe relationship with the person who is passing it on to you. You may not have an easy time at school, as cold facts and figures and logic are hard to grasp because there is no ready hook in your mind on which to hang them. This can make you appear inattentive and possibly even a slow or poor learner but your memory is, in fact, likely to be exceptionally retentive once you've formed some kind of personal relationship with incoming data. Pictures and diagrams, and stories about people's lives are better ways for you to learn, and you can be a gifted storyteller yourself.

Sun in Cancer with Mercury in Leo

Richard Branson   George W. Bush   Helen Keller
Nelson Mandela   Robin Williams   Marianne Williamson

You love to perform, and instinctively know just the right words and gestures that will create the perfect dramatic effect. Although rather bashful and shy, you've a desire to be noticed and an odd habit of pushing forward and stepping back at the same time. When the spotlight is on you, you're capable of stirring oratory. You impress listeners with the warmth and generosity of your personality and can help to lift their thoughts and spirits. Helen Keller, although blind and deaf, overcame her afflictions and, through her writings and stage appearances, inspired others to do the same. You learn best when you can see how what is being taught can be applied to you or your personal circumstances. It doesn't make much sense otherwise. Colourful stories and tales of honour and glory, especially about your own family or country, are what you can relate to and will bring out the best in you. Acting out, in your imagination or in real life – rather than acting on – information is your style. Sometimes fiction is the way you tell the truth.

You are fun to be around and you identify totally with

your beliefs. It can often be a case of love me, love what I am saying, with any disagreement taken as a sign of disloyalty. You could then sulk and withdraw if your ideas aren't roundly applauded so it is vital to avoid the tendency to surround yourself with 'yes men' to bolster up your opinions – and ego. It is much better to have a few good friends who will lovingly, but firmly, challenge you when you are straying off the point or getting stuck in a rut. Your leadership potential is great and you especially love putting heart into those you see as family.

NINE

Venus — At Your Pleasure

♀ THE GLYPH FOR VENUS IS MADE UP OF THE CIRCLE OF ETERNITY on top of the cross of matter. Esoterically this represents love, which is a quality of the divine, revealed on earth through personal choice. The saying 'One man's meat is another man's poison' couldn't be more relevant when it comes to what we love. It is a mystery why we find one thing attractive and another unattractive, or even repulsive. Looking at the sign, aspects and house of your Venus can't give any explanation of this mystery, but it can give some clear indications of what it is that you value and find desirable. This can be quite different from what current fashion tells you you should like. For example, many people are strongly turned on by voluptuous bodies but the media constantly shows images of near-anorexics as the desirable ideal. If you ignore what you, personally, find beautiful and try to be, or to love, what at heart leaves you cold, you are setting yourself up for unnecessary pain and dissatisfaction. Being true to your Venus sign, even if other people think you are strange, brings joy and pleasure. It also builds up your self-esteem because it grounds you solidly in your own personal values. This, in turn, makes you much more attractive to others. Not only that, it improves your relationships immeasurably, because you are living authentically and not betraying yourself by trying to prove your worth to others by being something you are not.

Glittering Venus, the brightest planet in the heavens, was named after the goddess of love, war and victory. Earlier names for her were Aphrodite, Innana and Ishtar. She was beautiful, self-willed and self-indulgent but was also skilled in all the arts of civilisation.

Your Venus sign shows what you desire and would like to possess, not only in relationships but also in all aspects of your taste, from clothes and culture to hobbies and hobby-horses. It identifies how and where you can be charming and seductive and skilful at creating your own type of beauty yourself. It also describes your style of attracting partners and the kind of people that turn you on. When your Venus is activated you feel powerful, desirable and wonderfully, wickedly indulged and indulgent. When it is not, even if someone has all the right credentials to make a good match, the relationship will always lack that certain something. If you don't take the chance to express your Venus to a good enough degree somewhere in your life, you miss out woefully on delight and happiness.

Morning Star, Evening Star

Venus appears in the sky either in the morning or in the evening. The ancients launched their attacks when Venus became a morning star, believing that she was then in her warrior-goddess role, releasing aggressive energy for victory in battle. If you're a morning-star person, you're likely to be impulsive, self-willed and idealistic, prepared to hold out until you find the partner who is just right for you.

Relationships and business dealings of morning-star Venus people are said to prosper best whenever Venus in the sky is a morning star. If you are an early bird, you can check this out. At these times Venus can be seen in the eastern sky before the Sun has risen.

The name for Venus as an evening star is Hesperus and it was then, traditionally, said to be sacred to lovers. Evening-star people tend to be easy-going and are open to negotiation, conciliation and making peace. If you are an evening-star Venus person, your best times in relationship and business affairs are said to be when Venus can be seen, jewel-like, in the western sky after the Sun has set.

Because the orbit of Venus is so close to the Sun, your Venus can only be in one of five signs. You have a morning-star Venus if your Venus is in one of the two signs that come before your Sun sign in the zodiac. You have an evening-star Venus if your Venus is in either of the two signs that follow your Sun sign. If you have Venus in the same sign as your Sun, you could be either, depending on whether your Venus is ahead of or behind your Sun. (You can find out which at the author's website www.janeridderpatrick.com.)

If you don't yet know your Venus sign, you might like to read through all of the following descriptions and see if you can guess what it is. You can find out for sure on pp. 116–18.

At the beginning of each section are the names of some well-known Cancerians with that particular Venus sign. You can find out more about them in Chapter Ten, Famous Cancer Birthdays.

Sun in Cancer with Venus in Taurus

Mel Brooks	Princess Diana	Imelda Marcos
Nancy Reagan	Prince William	The Duke of Windsor

Stability, both financial and emotional, is of the utmost importance to you. If you are feeling insecure, it can be all too easy for you to buy yourself pleasure and comfort by hitting the shops and collecting luxuries. Imelda Marcos, wife of the ousted President of the Philippines, was a notable big spender, with so many thousands of designer gowns, and shoes to match, that she could scarcely have had time to wear them all. Poverty, austerity and disruption do not suit you and even if you start off from deprived beginnings, you'll make it a priority to grow a fat bank balance and own your own home, which you'd love to fill with the finest the earth – or marketplace – can provide. With your shrewd business head and relentless determination, you'll quietly acquire all that you need for a comfortable life and a secure future for yourself and family.

You enjoy indulging your senses with good food and beautiful music. Sensual, satisfying sex can make a vital contribution to your emotional well-being. Without holding and caressing and spoiling, you simply wilt and, if neglected, you can become resentful and discontented. It can take you a while to commit but once you do, you are committed for life and, unless things go drastically wrong, are capable of great loyalty. Your worst nightmares are to be abandoned and to have your comfortable life disrupted. You may have to be careful not to try to control those you love and to allow them space to follow their own interests. Not only will this prevent your partner feeling stifled and confined; it will make your own life more interesting too.

Sun in Cancer with Venus in Gemini

Richard Branson   Jerry Hall   Courtney Love
George Michael   David Hockney   Mary Wesley

You love to keep up with the latest trends in whatever fields your interests lie. You are as sensitive to what is coming up on the mental horizon as to what is swirling around in the emotional environment. And you adore talking and gossiping and passing on the news and information to whoever you meet. This can make you a gifted communicator or writer – and possibly an incorrigible flirt. Keeping in touch with family and old acquaintances and making new ones gives you great pleasure, as you are more gregarious and sociable than most Cancerians. Being naturally sympathetic and approachable, people tend to feel safe with you and will pass on little titbits of gossip and personal information that others don't have access to.

You may also enjoy being in the news and talked about yourself – as long as what is being said is kind. A bad press can leave you feeling hurt and humiliated. You make a gifted mediator or go-between. Importantly, you also have the tact and sensitivity to know when to speak and when to keep silent, as well as the infinite patience and dogged determination to influence others into agreeing with your viewpoint.

Your definition of fidelity could be somewhat elastic or, alternatively, like Jerry Hall, you could be drawn to partners with wanderlust. To feel safe enough to be intimate, you need to bond with your partner intellectually, as well as emotionally, preferably with someone witty, clever and stimulating. Meeting new people and exploring new places at frequent intervals keeps you cheerful and content, so you need an understanding partner who will either accompany you or be relaxed about you getting out and about alone.

Sun in Cancer with Venus in Leo

Pamela Anderson	George W. Bush	Barbara Cartland
Antoni Gaudí	Tom Cruise	The Dalai Lama

Behind that shy and often retiring exterior lurks a powerful need to shine. This can range from the determination to be someone important in the eyes of the world, to achieving inner aristocracy like the Dalai Lama, so that you can pour out your generosity of spirit for the benefit of all. You are almost invariably fun to be with. Having such strong principles about love and loyalty, your preference is for honourable and upright behaviour. If you've pledged yourself in a relationship, you're unlikely to stray. It's hard for you to give up on a partnership once you are committed, because you pour so much of yourself into creating and shaping it. When your heart is not touched, though, you could be tempted to use others as elbow and ego decorations.

You are attracted to the best, and may even consider yourself a cut above the rest, becoming hurt and sulky if you are overlooked. You're in love with love and adore all of the trappings of romance – red roses and champagne and luxurious weekends away. With Leo around, the motto is often 'if you've got it, flaunt it', whether this is money, power or – like Pamela Anderson – curvaceous borders, and you may have to curb a tendency to spend irresponsibly. Opulence and extravagance turn you on. Antoni Gaudí's lavishly ornamented buildings in Barcelona are some of the wonders of the modern world; and Barbara Cartland, writer of reality-defying romantic fiction, was once called 'an animated meringue' because of her eye-popping personal decoration in the pink frou-frou style. Perhaps you are one of the quieter varieties, though, with refined good taste, cultivating integrity and inspiring leadership.

Sun in Cancer with Venus in Virgo

Edgar Degas   Sue Lawley   Iris Murdoch
Marcel Proust   Terence Stamp Robin Williams

You take great pride in doing things properly, as you love to be skilful at whatever you do — and to be of service. Being so fastidious about whom and what you have in your personal space, you can be rather critical of those who do not come up to your exactingly high standards. Writers, actors and artists with this combination take great pride in getting the details right, constantly upgrading their expertise and perfecting their craft. Marcel Proust preferred to hide himself away in a soundproof room and pay meticulous attention to the details of his inner life, and left the world some of the finest literature ever written.

You are likely to run your home — or your mind or body — in an efficient and orderly fashion, and may have an interest in health and hygiene. This can serve your family well, as long as you don't let it take over — Cancer and Virgo both have a tendency towards needless anxiety. There can be some tension between your need for intimacy and your pleasure in being alone. It's important that you allow space for both in your life. Resisting the temptation to fuss over your partner, trying to correct his or her faults, could prevent major problems in your relationships. As you can spot a flaw at a hundred paces, it may seem a pity not to use the information, but there are things that are best left well alone unless help has been requested. Some with this combination have inhibitions around sexual contact, being almost phobic about contagion and keeping obsessively clean, but when you do let your hair down, your senses take over and you can be wildly unrestrained to the point of abandonment.

TEN

Famous Cancer Birthdays

FIND OUT WHO SHARES YOUR MOON, MERCURY AND VENUS SIGNS, and any challenging Sun aspects, and see what they have done with the material they were born with. Notice how often it is not just the personalities of the people themselves but the roles of actors, characters of authors and works of artists that reflect their astrological make-up. In reading standard biographies, I've been constantly astounded – and, of course, delighted – at how often phrases used to describe individuals could have been lifted straight from their astrological profiles. Check it out yourself!

A few people below have been given a choice of two Moons. This is because the Moon changed sign on the day that they were born and no birth time was available. You may be able to guess which one is correct if you read the descriptions of the Moon signs in Chapter Seven.

21 June

1982 Prince William, son of Prince Charles and Diana, Princess of Wales
Sun aspects: Neptune
Moon: Cancer   Mercury: Gemini   Venus: Taurus

22 June

1940 Esther Rantzen, TV personality and founder of ChildLine for children in trouble or danger
Sun aspects: Neptune
Moon: Aquarius   Mercury: Cancer   Venus: Cancer

23 June

1894 King Edward VIII, who abdicated to marry American divorcee, Wallis Simpson, and became the Duke of Windsor
Sun aspects: none
Moon: Pisces   Mercury: Cancer   Venus: Taurus

June 24

1842 Ambrose Bierce, writer of sardonic humour, *The Devil's Dictionary*
Sun aspects: Saturn, Uranus
Moon: Capricorn   Mercury: Cancer   Venus: Leo

25 June

1852 Antoni Gaudí, architect of extravagantly ornate buildings in Barcelona
Sun aspects: none
Moon: Libra   Mercury: Gemini   Venus: Leo

26 June

1914 Laurie Lee, English poet and writer of *Cider with Rosie*

Sun aspects: Pluto
Moon: Leo   Mercury: Cancer   Venus: Leo

27 June
1880 Helen Keller, deaf and blind writer, scholar and inspirer of disabled people
Sun aspects: none
Moon: Pisces   Mercury: Leo   Venus: Cancer

28 June
1491 King Henry VIII, English king with six wives and an imperious will
Sun aspects: Uranus
Moon: Aries   Mercury: Leo   Venus: Gemini

29 June
1900 Antoine de St Exupéry, author and pilot, *The Little Prince*
Sun aspects: Saturn
Moon: Leo   Mercury: Leo   Venus: Cancer

30 June
1966 Mike Tyson, ear-biting American boxing champion, convicted of rape
Sun aspects: Saturn
Moon: Sagittarius   Mercury: Leo   Venus: Gemini

1 July
1961 Diana, Princess of Wales, 'The People's Princess'
Sun aspects: none
Moon: Aquarius   Mercury: Cancer   Venus: Taurus

2 July
1877 Hermann Hesse, Swiss author, *Steppenwolf, The Glass Bead Game*
Sun aspects: none
Moon: Pisces   Mercury: Gemini   Venus: Cancer

3 July
1728 Robert Adam, Scottish architect of romantically elegant, classical buildings
Sun aspects: none
Moon: Libra   Mercury: Leo   Venus: Cancer

4 July
1845 Thomas Barnardo, founder of Barnardo's Homes for destitute children
Sun aspects: Uranus
Moon: Cancer   Mercury: Cancer   Venus: Cancer

5 July
1810 P.T. Barnum, flamboyant and wealthy showman and circus-owner
Sun aspects: none
Moon: Leo   Mercury: Gemini   Venus: Leo

6 July
1935 The Dalai Lama, spiritual leader of the Tibetan people
Sun aspects: none
Moon: Virgo   Mercury: Gemini   Venus: Leo

7 July
1887 Marc Chagall, surrealist painter, juxtaposing animals and dream objects
Sun aspects: Saturn, Uranus
Moon: Aquarius   Mercury: Leo   Venus: Virgo

8 July
1926 Elisabeth Kübler-Ross, researcher in dying, *On Death and Dying*
Sun aspects: Pluto
Moon: Cancer   Mercury: Leo   Venus: Gemini

9 July
1901 Barbara Cartland, prolific romantic fiction writer and health food promoter
Sun aspects: Saturn
Moon: Aries   Mercury: Cancer   Venus: Leo

10 July
1871 Marcel Proust, reclusive introspective writer, *In Search of Lost Time*
Sun aspects: Uranus, Neptune
Moon: Taurus   Mercury: Cancer   Venus: Virgo

11 July
1934 Giorgio Armani, trend-setting Italian fashion designer
Sun aspects: Pluto
Moon: Cancer   Mercury: Cancer   Venus: Gemini

12 July
1817 Henry David Thoreau, American writer, *Walden, or Life in the Woods*
Sun aspects: none
Moon: Cancer   Mercury: Cancer   Venus: Gemini

13 July
1527 John Dee, alchemist, astrologer and spy for Queen Elizabeth I
Sun aspects: Saturn, Pluto
Moon: Capricorn   Mercury: Cancer   Venus: Virgo

14 July
1858 Emmeline Pankhurst, militant English suffragette
Sun aspects: Saturn
Moon: Virgo   Mercury: Cancer   Venus: Leo

15 July
1919 Iris Murdoch, Irish novelist and philosopher, *The Sea, The Sea*
Sun aspects: none
Moon: Aquarius   Mercury: Leo   Venus: Virgo

16 July
1821 Mary Baker Eddy, founder of the First Church of Christ, scientist
Sun aspects: Saturn
Moon: Aquarius   Mercury: Leo   Venus: Leo

17 July
1947 Camilla Parker Bowles, companion of Prince Charles
Sun aspects: none
Moon: Cancer   Mercury: Cancer   Venus: Cancer

18 July
1918 Nelson Mandela, South African President after spending 29 years in jail
Sun aspects: none
Moon: Scorpio   Mercury: Leo   Venus: Gemini

19 July
1834 Edgar Degas, reclusive French painter, especially of ballet dancers
Sun aspects: Neptune
Moon: Capricorn   Mercury: Leo   Venus: Virgo

20 July
1919 Sir Edmund Hillary, first mountaineer to reach the summit of Mount Everest
Sun aspects: none
Moon: Aries   Mercury: Leo   Venus: Virgo

21 July
1899 Ernest Hemingway, author, *A Farewell to Arms, For Whom the Bell Tolls*
Sun aspects: none
Moon: Capricorn   Mercury: Leo   Venus: Cancer

22 July
1822 Gregor Mendel, Austrian priest and scientist, father of modern genetics
Sun aspects: none
Moon: Virgo   Mercury: Cancer   Venus: Gemini

23 July
1936 Richard Bach, author of bestseller *Jonathan Livingstone Seagull*
Sun aspects: Saturn
Moon: Leo   Mercury: Gemini   Venus: Cancer

Other Cancer people mentioned in this book
Isabelle Adjani, actress, *Toxic Affair* ☆ Roald Amundsen, first person to reach the South Pole ☆ Pamela Anderson, actress, *Baywatch* ☆ Arthur Ashe, first male black tennis player to reach world ranking ☆ Kathy Bates, actress, *Misery* ☆ John Bradshaw, therapist, *Home Coming: Reclaiming & Championing Your Inner Child* ☆ Richard Branson, entrepreneur ☆ Anita Brookner, author, *Hôtel du Lac* ☆ Mel Brooks, film director, *Blazing Saddles* ☆ Julie Burchill, newspaper columnist ☆ George W. Bush, US president ☆ Diahann

Carroll, actress and singer, *Dynasty* ☆ Judy Chicago, artist and feminist, *The Dinner Party* ☆ Wendy Cope, poet, *Never Trust a Journalist* ☆ Tom Cruise, actor, *Mission Impossible* ☆ John Cusack, actor, *Being John Malkovich* ☆ Trevor Eve, actor, *Raising the Dead* ☆ Dianne Feinstein, US senator and former Mayor of San Francisco ☆ Gerald Ford, US president ☆ Harrison Ford, actor, *Star Wars* ☆ Rodolfo Gucci, Italian fashion designer ☆ Jerry Hall, model and partner of Mick Jagger ☆ Tom Hanks, actor, *Saving Private Ryan* ☆ Olivia de Havilland, actress, *Gone with the Wind* ☆ Nathaniel Hawthorne, author, *The Scarlet Letter* ☆ Edward Heath, British prime minister, yachtsman and musician ☆ Myra Hindley, child-murderer ☆ David Hockney, artist best known for his 'swimming pool' paintings ☆ Franz Kafka, author, *The Castle*, *The Trial* ☆ Frida Kahlo, Mexican artist ☆ Lord Kitchener, Irish statesman and army-recruiter ☆ Gustav Klimt, artist, *The Kiss* ☆ Käthe Kollwitz, German artist and political activist ☆ Estée Lauder, founder of cosmetic empire ☆ Sue Lawley, radio presenter, *Desert Island Discs* ☆ Ellen MacArthur, intrepid yachtswoman ☆ Imelda Marcos, extravagant wife of deposed Phillipines President ☆ Paul Merton, radio and TV personality and wit ☆ George Michael, singer, *Faith* ☆ Lord Louis Mountbatten, last viceroy of India, murdered by the IRA ☆ George Orwell, author, *Animal Farm*, *1984* ☆ Mervyn Peake, author, *Gormenghast* ☆ Nancy Reagan, wife of former US president Ronald Reagan ☆ Diana Rigg, actress, *The Avengers* ☆ Ginger Rogers, actress and dancer with Fred Astaire ☆ Donald Rumsfeld, US defence secretary ☆ George Sand, prolific French writer and lover of Chopin ☆ Carly Simon, singer, 'You're So Vain' ☆ Terence Stamp, actor, *The Collector* ☆ Cat Stevens, singer and convert to Islam, 'Peace Train' ☆ Kenneth Starr, US attorney and Special Prosecutor of Bill Clinton ☆ Meryl Streep, actress, *Out of Africa* ☆ Liv Tyler, actress, *The Lord of the Rings* ☆ John Wesley, evangelist and founder of Methodism ☆ Mary Wesley, author who published her first book aged 70, *The Camomile Lawn* ☆ Richard Wilson, actor, Victor Meldrew in *One Foot in the Grave* ☆ Robin Williams, actor, *Dead Poets Society* ☆ Marianne Williamson, inspirational speaker and writer, *A Return to Love* ☆ Colin Wilson, author, *Origins of the Sexual Impulse*, *The Occult* ☆ Natalie Wood, actress, *West Side Story*

ELEVEN

Finding Your Sun, Moon, Mercury and Venus Signs

ALL OF THE ASTROLOGICAL DATA IN THIS BOOK WAS CALCULATED by Astrolabe, who also supply a wide range of astrological software. I am most grateful for their help and generosity.

ASTROLABE, PO Box 1750, Brewster, MA 02631, USA
www.alabe.com

PLEASE NOTE THAT ALL OF THE TIMES GIVEN ARE IN GREENWICH MEAN TIME (GMT). If you were born during British Summer Time (BST) you will need to subtract one hour from your birth time to convert it to GMT. If you were born outside of the British Isles, find the time zone of your place of birth and the number of hours it is different from GMT. Add the difference in hours if you were born west of the UK, and subtract the difference if you were born east of the UK to convert your birth time to GMT.

Your Sun Sign

Check your year of birth, and if you were born between the dates and times given the Sun was in Cancer when you were born – confirming that you're a Cancer. If you were born before the time on the date that Cancer begins in your year, you are a Gemini. If you were born after the time on the date Cancer ends in your year, you are a Leo.

Your Moon Sign

The Moon changes sign every two and a half days. To find your Moon sign, first find your year of birth. You will notice that in each year box there are three columns.

The second column shows the day of the month that the Moon changed sign, while the first column gives the abbreviation for the sign that the Moon entered on that date.

In the middle column, the month has been omitted, so that the dates run from, for example, 21 to 30 (June) and then from 1 to 23 (July).

In the third column, after the star, the time that the Moon changed sign on that day is given.

Look down the middle column of your year box to find your date of birth. If your birth date is given, look to the third column to find the time that the Moon changed sign. If you were born after that time, your Moon sign is given in the first column next to your birth date. If you were born before that time, your Moon sign is the one above the one next to your birth date.

If your birth date is not given, find the closest date before it. The sign shown next to that date is your Moon sign.

If you were born on a day that the Moon changed signs and you do not know your time of birth, try out both of that day's Moon signs and feel which one fits you best.

The abbreviations for the signs are as follows:

Aries – Ari   Taurus – Tau   Gemini – Gem   Cancer – Can
Leo – Leo   Virgo – Vir   Libra – Lib   Scorpio – Sco
Sagittarius – Sag   Capricorn – Cap   Aquarius – Aqu   Pisces – Pis

Your Mercury Sign

Find your year of birth and then the column in which your birthday falls. Look up to the top of the column to find your Mercury sign. You will see that some dates appear twice. This is because Mercury changed sign that day. If your birthday falls on one of these dates, try out both Mercury signs and see which one fits you best. If you know your birth time, you can find out for sure which Mercury sign is yours on my website – www.janeridderpatrick.com.

Your Venus Sign

Find your year of birth and then the column in which your birthday falls. Look up to the top of the column to find your Venus sign. Some dates have two possible signs. That's because Venus changed signs that day. Try them both out and see which fits you best. If the year you are interested in doesn't appear in the tables, or you have Venus in the same sign as your Sun and want to know whether you have a morning or evening star Venus, you can find the information on my website – www.janeridderpatrick.com.

♋ Cancer Sun Tables ☉

YEAR	Cancer Begins	Cancer Ends
1930	22 Jun 03.52	23 Jul 14.42
1931	22Jun 09.28	23 Jul 20.21
1932	21 Jun 15.22	23 Jul 02.18
1933	21 Jun 21.11	23 Jul 08.05
1934	22 Jun 02.47	23 Jul 13.42
1935	22 Jun 08.37	23 Jul 19.32
1936	21 Jun 14.21	23 Jul 01.17
1937	21 Jun 20.12	23 Jul 07.06
1938	22 Jun 02.03	23 Jul 12.57
1939	22 Jun 07.39	23 Jul 18.36
1940	21 Jun13.36	23 Jul 00.34
1941	21 Jun 19.33	23 Jul 06.26
1942	22 Jun 01.16	23 Jul 12.07
1943	22 Jun 07.12	23 Jul 18.04
1944	21 Jun 13.02	22 Jul 23.55
1945	21 Jun 18.52	23 Jul 05.45
1946	22 Jun 00.44	23 Jul 11.37
1947	22 Jun 06.18	23 Jul 17.14
1948	21 Jun 12.10	22 Jul 23.07
1949	21 Jun 18.02	23 Jul 04.56
1950	21 Jun 23.36	23 Jul 10.29
1951	22 Jun 05.24	23 Jul 16.20
1952	21 Jun 11.12	22 Jul 22.07
1953	21 Jun 16.59	23 Jul 03.52
1954	21 Jun 22.54	23 Jul 09.44
1955	22 Jun 04.31	23 Jul 15.24
1956	21 Jun 10.23	22 Jul 21.19
1957	21 Jun 16.20	23 Jun 03.14
1958	21 Jun 21.56	23 Jul 08.50
1959	22 Jun 03.49	23 Jul 14.45
1960	21 Jun 09.42	22 Jul 20.37
1961	21 Jun 15.30	23 Jul 02.23
1962	21 Jun 21.24	23 Jul 08.17
1963	22 Jun 03.04	23 Jul 13.59

YEAR	Cancer Begins	Cancer Ends
1964	21 Jun 08.56	22 Jul 19.52
1965	21 Jun 14.55	23 Jul 01.48
1966	21 Jun 20.33	23 Jul 07.23
1967	22 Jun 02.22	23 Jul 13.15
1968	21 Jun 08.13	22 Jul 19.07
1969	21 Jun 13.55	23 Jul 00.48
1970	21 Jun 19.42	23 Jul 06.36
1971	22 Jun 01.19	23 Jul 12.14
1972	21 Jun 07.06	22 Jul 18.02
1973	21 Jun 13.00	22 Jul 23.55
1974	21 Jun 18.37	23 Jul 05.30
1975	22 Jun 00.26	23 Jul 11.21
1976	21 Jun 06.24	22 Jul 17.18
1977	21 Jun 12.13	22 Jul 23.03
1978	21 Jun 18.09	23 Jul 05.00
1979	21 Jun 23.56	23 Jul 10.48
1980	21 Jun 05.47	22 Jul 16.41
1981	21 Jun 11.44	22 Jul 22.39
1982	21 Jun 17.23	23 Jul 04.15
1983	21 Jun 23.08	23 Jul 10.04
1984	21 Jun 05.02	22 Jul 15.58
1985	21 Jun 10.44	22 Jul 21.36
1986	21 Jun 16.29	23 Jul 03.24
1987	21 Jun 22.10	23 Jul 09.06
1988	21 Jun 03.56	22 Jul 14.51
1989	21 Jun 09.53	22 Jul 20.45
1990	21 Jun 15.32	23 Jul 02.21
1991	21 Jun 21.28	23 Jul 08.11
1992	21 Jun 03.14	22 Jul 14.08
1993	21 Jun 08.59	22 Jul 19.50
1994	21 Jun 14.47	23 Jul 01.40
1995	21 Jun 20.34	23 Jul 07.29
1996	21 Jun 02.23	22 Jul 13.18
1997	21 Jun 08.19	22 Jul 19.15
1998	21 Jun 14.02	23 Jul 00.55
1999	21 Jun 19.49	23 Jul 06.44
2000	21 Jun 01.47	22 Jul 12.42

♋ Cancer – Finding Your Moon Sign ☽

1930		
Tau	21	*23:33
Gem	24	*04:59
Can	26	*06:57
Leo	28	*07:06
Vir	30	*07:28
Lib	2	*09:48
Sco	4	*14:56
Sag	6	*22:49
Cap	9	*08:49
Acu	11	*20:22
Pis	14	*08:57
Ari	16	*21:25
Tau	19	*07:53
Gem	21	*14:37

1931		
Lib	22	*23:22
Sco	25	*02:34
Sag	27	*06:26
Cap	29	*11:35
Aqu	1	*18:56
Pis	4	*05:09
Ari	6	*17:39
Tau	9	*06:13
Gem	11	*16:13
Can	13	*22:29
Leo	16	*01:40
Vir	18	*03:21
Lib	20	*05:06
Sco	22	*07:56

1932		
Pis	23	*02:26
Ari	25	*12:34
Tau	28	*01:07
Gem	30	*13:34
Can	3	*00:05
Leo	5	*08:17
Vir	7	*14:32
Lib	9	*19:12
Sco	11	*22:27
Sag	14	*00:37
Cap	16	*02:35
Aqu	18	*05:44
Pis	20	*11:35
Ari	22	*20:52

1933		
Can	22	*23:06
Leo	25	*11:16
Vir	27	*22:00
Lib	30	*06:10
Sco	2	*10:55
Sag	4	*12:30
Cap	6	*12:15
Aqu	8	*12:05
Pis	10	*14:02
Ari	12	*19:31
Tau	15	*04:49
Gem	17	*16:44
Can	20	*05:24
Leo	22	*17:18

1934		
Sco	22	*17:24
Sag	24	*20:48
Cap	26	*21:23
Aqu	28	*21:02
Pis	30	*21:38
Ari	3	*00:39
Tau	5	*06:47
Gem	7	*15:55
Can	10	*03:20
Leo	12	*16:07
Vir	15	*05:06
Lib	17	*16:46
Sco	20	*01:29
Sag	22	*06:27

69 Cancer – Finding Your Moon Sign ☽

1935		
Pis	21	*09:55
Ari	23	*12:21
Tau	25	*15:54
Gem	27	*21:06
Can	30	*04:26
Leo	2	*14:13
Vir	5	*02:08
Lib	7	*14:52
Sco	10	*02:14
Sag	12	*10:26
Cap	14	*15:01
Aqu	16	*16:53
Pis	18	*17:30
Ari	20	*18:32

1936		
Leo	21	*14:06
Vir	23	*22:16
Lib	26	*09:23
Sco	28	*21:52
Sag	1	*09:26
Cap	3	*18:33
Aqu	6	*00:55
Pis	8	*05:10
Ari	10	*08:09
Tau	12	*10:45
Gem	14	*13:38
Can	16	*17:27
Leo	18	*22:58
Vir	21	*06:53

1937		
Sag	21	*06:25
Cap	23	*18:57
Aqu	26	*05:53
Pis	28	*14:35
Ari	30	*20:49
Tau	3	*00:33
Gem	5	*02:14
Can	7	*02:53
Leo	9	*03:59
Vir	11	*07:15
Lib	13	*14:05
Sco	16	*00:36
Sag	18	*13:20
Cap	21	*01:49

1938		
Ari	21	*03:38
Tau	23	*09:48
Gem	25	*12:23
Can	27	*12:26
Leo	29	*11:45
Vir	1	*12:24
Lib	3	*16:09
Sco	5	*23:49
Sag	8	*10:45
Cap	10	*23:21
Aqu	13	*12:05
Pis	15	*23:54
Ari	18	*10:01
Tau	20	*17:30

1939		
Vir	21	*22:56
Lib	24	*01:31
Sco	26	*06:25
Sag	28	*13:39
Cap	30	*22:53
Aqu	3	*09:54
Pis	5	*22:17
Ari	8	*10:49
Tau	10	*21:25
Gem	13	*04:19
Can	15	*07:15
Leo	17	*07:30
Vir	19	*07:07
Lib	21	*08:10

♋ Cancer – Finding Your Moon Sign ☽

1940		
Aqu	22	*08:15
Pis	24	*17:55
Ari	27	*06:12
Tau	29	*18:52
Gem	2	*05:14
Can	4	*12:09
Leo	6	*16:11
Vir	8	*18:44
Lib	10	*21:06
Sco	13	*00:07
Sag	15	*04:04
Cap	17	*09:18
Aqu	19	*16:22
Pis	22	*01:58

1941		
Gem	22	*02:43
Can	24	*13:50
Leo	26	*22:54
Vir	29	*06:02
Lib	1	*11:16
Sco	3	*14:32
Sag	5	*16:13
Cap	7	*17:20
Aqu	9	*19:36
Pis	12	*00:43
Ari	14	*09:35
Tau	16	*21:29
Gem	19	*10:09
Can	21	*21:14

1942		
Lib	21	*21:03
Sco	24	*01:49
Sag	26	*03:08
Cap	28	*02:29
Aqu	30	*02:01
Pis	2	*03:46
Ari	4	*09:11
Tau	6	*18:22
Gem	9	*06:10
Can	11	*18:51
Leo	14	*07:07
Vir	16	*18:08
Lib	19	*03:01
Sco	21	*09:01

1943		
Pis	22	*12:37
Ari	24	*15:53
Tau	26	*21:52
Gem	29	*06:26
Can	1	*17:13
Leo	4	*05:39
Vir	6	*18:44
Lib	9	*06:43
Sco	11	*15:39
Sag	13	*20:35
Cap	15	*22:05
Aqu	17	*21:45
Pis	19	*21:31
Ari	21	*23:09

1944		
Leo	23	*03:26
Vir	25	*14:58
Lib	28	*03:39
Sco	30	*15:09
Sag	2	*23:36
Cap	5	*04:41
Aqu	7	*07:13
Pis	9	*08:38
Ari	11	*10:18
Tau	13	*13:16
Gem	15	*18:11
Can	18	*01:22
Leo	20	*10:51
Vir	22	*22:24

1945

Sag	22	*22:26
Cap	25	*08:13
Aqu	27	*15:35
Pis	29	*20:50
Ari	2	*00:28
Tau	4	*03:04
Gem	6	*05:19
Can	8	*08:10
Leo	10	*12:44
Vir	12	*19:58
Lib	15	*06:12
Sco	17	*18:28
Sag	20	*06:35
Cap	22	*16:28

1946

Ari	22	*12:18
Tau	24	*15:55
Gem	26	*17:07
Can	28	*17:10
Leo	30	*17:47
Vir	2	*20:45
Lib	5	*03:21
Sco	7	*13:42
Sag	10	*02:20
Cap	12	*15:05
Aqu	15	*02:16
Pis	17	*11:14
Ari	19	*17:58
Tau	21	*22:34

1947

Leo	21	*02:06
Vir	23	*03:01
Lib	25	*06:51
Sco	27	*14:17
Sag	30	*00:46
Cap	2	*13:02
Aqu	5	*01:49
Pis	7	*14:02
Ari	10	*00:33
Tau	12	*08:11
Gem	14	*12:15
Can	16	*13:13
Leo	18	*12:34
Vir	20	*12:20
Lib	22	*14:34

1948

Cap	21	*12:51
Aqu	23	*23:15
Pis	26	*11:23
Ari	28	*23:55
Tau	1	*10:38
Gem	3	*17:47
Can	5	*21:05
Leo	7	*21:52
Vir	9	*22:04
Lib	11	*23:31
Sco	14	*03:28
Sag	16	*10:11
Cap	18	*19:13
Aqu	21	*06:02

1949

Tau	21	*07:29
Gem	23	*18:19
Can	26	*02:00
Leo	28	*07:00
Vir	30	*10:26
Lib	2	*13:21
Sco	4	*16:21
Sag	6	*19:45
Cap	9	*00:02
Aqu	11	*06:08
Pis	13	*15:02
Ari	16	*02:43
Tau	18	*15:35
Gem	21	*02:56

1950			1951			1952			1953			1954		
Lib	23	*03:08	Aqu	21	*16:04	Can	22	*07:04	Sco	22	*03:56	Pis	21	*12:35
Sco	25	*06:18	Pis	23	*17:49	Leo	24	*19:02	Sag	24	*12:46	Ari	23	*16:43
Sag	27	*07:25	Ari	25	*23:14	Vir	27	*08:05	Cap	26	*18:28	Tau	25	*19:08
Cap	29	*07:48	Tau	28	*08:17	Lib	29	*20:17	Aqu	28	*21:50	Gem	27	*20:41
Aqu	1	*09:20	Gem	30	*19:51	Sco	2	*05:24	Pis	1	*00:08	Can	29	*22:36
Pis	3	*13:52	Can	3	*08:27	Sag	4	*10:25	Ari	3	*02:23	Leo	2	*02:17
Ari	5	*22:25	Leo	5	*21:00	Cap	6	*12:01	Tau	5	*05:23	Vir	4	*08:56
Tau	8	*10:13	Vir	8	*08:35	Aqu	8	*11:54	Gem	7	*09:42	Lib	6	*18:53
Gem	10	*23:01	Lib	10	*18:04	Pis	10	*11:59	Can	9	*15:54	Sco	9	*07:03
Can	13	*10:32	Sco	13	*00:17	Ari	12	*13:57	Leo	12	*00:28	Sag	11	*19:18
Leo	15	*19:51	Sag	15	*03:02	Tau	14	*18:45	Vir	14	*11:28	Cap	14	*05:39
Vir	18	*03:04	Cap	17	*03:13	Gem	17	*02:38	Lib	17	*00:03	Aqu	16	*13:18
Lib	20	*08:33	Aqu	19	*02:41	Can	19	*13:05	Sco	19	*12:15	Pis	18	*18:32
Sco	22	*12:26	Pis	21	*03:29	Leo	22	*01:20	Sag	21	*21:57	Ari	20	*22:06

♋ Cancer – Finding Your Moon Sign ☽

1955		
Leo	22	*07:36
Vir	24	*10:27
Lib	26	*16:55
Sco	29	*03:04
Sag	1	*15:34
Cap	4	*04:29
Aqu	6	*16:17
Pis	9	*02:07
Ari	11	*09:32
Tau	13	*14:19
Gem	15	*16:42
Can	17	*17:29
Leo	19	*18:03
Vir	21	*20:06

1956		
Cap	23	*02:43
Aqu	25	*15:25
Pis	28	*03:54
Ari	30	*14:41
Tau	2	*22:24
Gem	5	*02:24
Can	7	*03:19
Leo	9	*02:42
Vir	11	*02:35
Lib	13	*04:54
Sco	15	*10:57
Sag	17	*20:38
Cap	20	*08:40
Aqu	22	*21:28

1957		
Tau	22	*23:36
Gem	25	*07:06
Can	27	*10:59
Leo	29	*12:30
Vir	1	*13:23
Lib	3	*15:16
Sco	5	*19:10
Sag	8	*01:20
Cap	10	*09:35
Aqu	12	*19:43
Pis	15	*07:32
Ari	17	*20:14
Tau	20	*07:57
Gem	22	*16:33

1958		
Vir	22	*02:21
Lib	24	*05:42
Sco	26	*08:30
Sag	28	*11:11
Cap	30	*14:32
Aqu	2	*19:44
Pis	5	*03:57
Ari	7	*15:18
Tau	10	*04:08
Gem	12	*15:45
Can	15	*00:14
Leo	17	*05:30
Vir	19	*08:41
Lib	21	*11:11

1959		
Aqu	22	*23:01
Pis	25	*03:13
Ari	27	*11:23
Tau	29	*23:11
Gem	2	*12:05
Can	5	*00:02
Leo	7	*10:07
Vir	9	*18:15
Lib	12	*00:25
Sco	14	*04:32
Sag	16	*06:41
Cap	18	*07:41
Aqu	20	*09:05
Pis	22	*12:42

♋ Cancer – Finding Your Moon Sign ☽

1960			1961			1962			1963			1964		
Gem	21	*09:46	Lib	21	*09:30	Pis	22	*15:58	Can	21	*12:47	Sag	22	*05:03
Can	23	*22:09	Sco	23	*18:50	Ari	24	*18:42	Leo	23	*15:44	Cap	24	*18:01
Leo	26	*10:51	Sag	26	*00:04	Tau	26	*21:34	Vir	25	*21:57	Aqu	27	*06:21
Vir	28	*22:52	Cap	28	*01:58	Gem	29	*01:09	Lib	28	*07:40	Pis	29	*16:55
Lib	1	*08:45	Aqu	30	*02:17	Can	1	*06:18	Sco	30	*19:47	Ari	2	*00:51
Sco	3	*15:07	Pis	2	*02:53	Leo	3	*13:56	Sag	3	*08:10	Tau	4	*05:42
Sag	5	*17:42	Ari	4	*05:12	Vir	6	*00:22	Cap	5	*19:02	Gem	6	*07:42
Cap	7	*17:34	Tau	6	*10:02	Lib	8	*12:47	Aqu	8	*03:35	Can	8	*07:56
Aqu	9	*16:43	Gem	8	*17:27	Sco	11	*01:04	Pis	10	*09:52	Leo	10	*08:01
Pis	11	*17:19	Can	11	*03:13	Sag	13	*10:59	Ari	12	*14:15	Vir	12	*09:45
Ari	13	*21:08	Leo	13	*14:56	Cap	15	*17:31	Tau	14	*17:14	Lib	14	*14:42
Tau	16	*04:48	Vir	16	*03:54	Aqu	17	*21:06	Gem	16	*19:27	Sco	16	*23:33
Gem	18	*15:40	Lib	18	*16:38	Pis	19	*22:59	Can	18	*21:45	Sag	19	*11:28
Can	21	*04:08	Sco	21	*03:03	Ari	22	*00:33	Leo	21	*01:15	Cap	22	*00:26

105

69 Cancer – Finding Your Moon Sign ☽

1965			1966			1967			1968			1969		
Ari	22	*04:28	Leo	21	*03:28	Cap	22	*04:46	Gem	23	*01:21	Lib	22	*23:02
Tau	24	*12:14	Vir	23	*05:07	Aqu	24	*09:11	Can	25	*13:42	Sco	25	*05:30
Gem	26	*16:17	Lib	25	*07:22	Pis	26	*16:49	Leo	28	*00:29	Sag	27	*07:59
Can	28	*17:19	Sco	27	*11:04	Ari	29	*03:52	Vir	30	*09:25	Cap	29	*07:44
Leo	30	*16:58	Sag	29	*16:31	Tau	1	*16:42	Lib	2	*16:09	Aqu	1	*06:49
Vir	2	*17:11	Cap	1	*23:51	Gem	4	*04:38	Sco	4	*20:19	Pis	3	*07:26
Lib	4	*19:43	Aqu	4	*09:14	Can	6	*13:46	Sag	6	*22:03	Ari	5	*11:17
Sco	7	*01:38	Pis	6	*20:39	Leo	8	*19:58	Cap	8	*22:23	Tau	7	*18:53
Sag	9	*10:54	Ari	9	*09:15	Vir	11	*00:07	Aqu	10	*23:04	Gem	10	*05:31
Cap	11	*22:29	Tau	11	*21:02	Lib	13	*03:19	Pis	13	*02:04	Can	12	*17:47
Aqu	14	*11:07	Gem	14	*05:51	Sco	15	*06:17	Ari	15	*08:52	Leo	15	*06:28
Pis	16	*23:44	Can	16	*10:43	Sag	17	*09:22	Tau	17	*19:30	Vir	17	*18:41
Ari	19	*11:11	Leo	18	*12:26	Cap	19	*12:59	Gem	20	*08:12	Lib	20	*05:19
Tau	21	*20:13	Vir	20	*12:46	Aqu	21	*17:59	Can	22	*20:30	Sco	22	*13:02
			Lib	22	*13:38									

♋ Cancer – Finding Your Moon Sign ☽

1970

Aqu	21	*17:00
Pis	23	*18:11
Ari	25	*20:52
Tau	28	*01:35
Gem	30	*08:24
Can	2	*17:20
Leo	5	*04:26
Vir	7	*17:10
Lib	10	*06:02
Sco	12	*16:40
Sag	14	*23:24
Cap	17	*02:18
Aqu	19	*02:44
Pis	21	*02:36

1971

Can	22	*20:30
Leo	25	*03:12
Vir	27	*13:06
Lib	30	*01:22
Sco	2	*13:45
Sag	4	*23:57
Cap	7	*07:02
Aqu	9	*11:25
Pis	11	*14:14
Ari	13	*16:32
Tau	15	*19:10
Gem	17	*22:47
Can	20	*03:56
Leo	22	*11:17

1972

Sco	21	*08:42
Sag	23	*21:13
Cap	26	*08:35
Aqu	28	*18:02
Pis	1	*01:17
Ari	3	*06:21
Tau	5	*09:24
Gem	7	*11:04
Can	9	*12:29
Leo	11	*15:05
Vir	13	*20:16
Lib	16	*04:49
Sco	18	*16:15
Sag	21	*04:46

1973

Pis	21	*07:28
Ari	23	*15:47
Tau	25	*20:36
Gem	27	*22:16
Can	29	*22:08
Leo	1	*21:56
Vir	3	*23:32
Lib	6	*04:24
Sco	8	*13:06
Sag	11	*00:47
Cap	13	*13:45
Aqu	16	*02:14
Pis	18	*13:06
Ari	20	*21:42

1974

Leo	22	*07:29
Vir	24	*08:11
Lib	26	*10:58
Sco	28	*16:40
Sag	1	*01:21
Cap	3	*12:19
Aqu	6	*00:41
Pis	8	*13:25
Ari	11	*01:09
Tau	13	*10:19
Gem	15	*15:53
Can	17	*17:56
Leo	19	*17:42
Vir	21	*17:09

69 Cancer – Finding Your Moon Sign ☽

1975		1976		1977		1978		1979	
Sag	21 *07:34	Tau	22 *05:21	Vir	22 *00:27	Aqu	22 *21:07	Gem	21 *23:23
Cap	23 *13:56	Gem	24 *17:36	Lib	24 *07:34	Pis	24 *21:57	Can	24 *07:24
Aqu	25 *22:33	Can	27 *03:28	Sco	26 *11:40	Ari	27 *01:54	Leo	26 *17:46
Pis	28 *09:33	Leo	29 *10:38	Sag	28 *13:01	Tau	29 *09:21	Vir	29 *06:13
Ari	30 *22:01	Vir	1 *15:45	Cap	30 *12:48	Gem	1 *19:37	Lib	1 *19:07
Tau	3 *09:53	Lib	3 *19:34	Aqu	2 *12:57	Can	4 *07:33	Sco	4 *05:57
Gem	5 *18:58	Sco	5 *22:33	Pis	4 *15:31	Leo	6 *20:12	Sag	6 *12:54
Can	8 *00:21	Sag	8 *01:05	Ari	6 *22:04	Vir	9 *08:44	Cap	8 *16:06
Leo	10 *02:49	Cap	10 *03:49	Tau	9 *08:33	Lib	11 *19:47	Aqu	10 *16:58
Vir	12 *03:55	Aqu	12 *07:53	Gem	11 *21:14	Sco	14 *03:45	Pis	12 *17:22
Lib	14 *05:21	Pis	14 *14:36	Can	14 *09:49	Sag	16 *07:48	Ari	14 *18:57
Sco	16 *08:23	Ari	17 *00:40	Leo	16 *20:50	Cap	18 *08:32	Tau	16 *22:43
Sag	18 *13:32	Tau	19 *13:11	Vir	19 *05:58	Aqu	20 *07:41	Gem	19 *04:59
Cap	20 *20:46	Gem	22 *01:39	Lib	21 *13:08	Pis	22 *07:26	Can	21 *13:40

♋ Cancer – Finding Your Moon Sign ☽

1980		
Sco	23	*02:25
Sag	25	*13:00
Cap	27	*20:45
Aqu	30	*02:03
Pis	1	*05:48
Ari	4	*08:46
Tau	6	*11:30
Gem	8	*14:33
Can	10	*18:44
Leo	13	*01:03
Vir	15	*10:11
Lib	17	*21:55
Sco	20	*10:32
Sag	22	*21:41

1981		
Pis	22	*16:43
Ari	24	*22:17
Tau	27	*01:15
Gem	29	*02:20
Can	1	*02:57
Leo	3	*04:47
Vir	5	*09:27
Lib	7	*17:42
Sco	10	*05:01
Sag	12	*17:34
Cap	15	*05:19
Aqu	17	*15:01
Pis	19	*22:24
Ari	22	*03:43

1982		
Can	21	*12:12
Leo	23	*11:57
Vir	25	*13:37
Lib	27	*18:30
Sco	30	*03:02
Sag	2	*14:25
Cap	5	*03:14
Aqu	7	*16:02
Pis	10	*03:34
Ari	12	*12:47
Tau	14	*18:59
Gem	16	*22:02
Can	18	*22:45
Leo	20	*22:35
Vir	22	*23:21

1983		
Sag	22	*15:55
Cap	25	*02:08
Aqu	27	*14:06
Pis	30	*02:51
Ari	2	*14:46
Tau	5	*00:03
Gem	7	*05:40
Can	9	*07:49
Leo	11	*07:53
Vir	13	*07:43
Lib	15	*09:10
Sco	17	*13:39
Sag	19	*21:32
Cap	22	*08:11

1984		
Ari	21	*10:40
Tau	23	*22:37
Gem	26	*08:03
Can	28	*14:08
Leo	30	*17:29
Vir	2	*19:27
Lib	4	*21:26
Sco	7	*00:28
Sag	9	*05:03
Cap	11	*11:23
Aqu	13	*19:41
Pis	16	*06:10
Ari	18	*18:25
Tau	21	*06:52

♋ Cancer – Finding Your Moon Sign ☽

1985		
Leo	21	*01:31
Vir	23	*07:32
Lib	25	*11:46
Sco	27	*14:36
Sag	29	*16:30
Cap	1	*18:22
Aqu	3	*21:36
Pis	6	*03:40
Ari	8	*13:21
Tau	11	*01:44
Gem	13	*14:22
Can	16	*00:53
Leo	18	*08:24
Vir	20	*13:28
Lib	22	*17:09

1986		
Cap	22	*02:59
Aqu	24	*02:50
Pis	26	*05:12
Ari	28	*11:35
Tau	30	*21:54
Gem	3	*10:31
Can	5	*23:18
Leo	8	*10:55
Vir	10	*20:49
Lib	13	*04:39
Sco	15	*09:57
Sag	17	*12:33
Cap	19	*13:09
Aqu	21	*13:18

1987		
Tau	21	*00:09
Gem	23	*09:54
Can	25	*21:22
Leo	28	*09:52
Vir	30	*22:33
Lib	3	*09:53
Sco	5	*18:02
Sag	7	*22:03
Cap	9	*22:42
Aqu	11	*21:49
Pis	13	*21:36
Ari	16	*00:01
Tau	18	*06:04
Gem	20	*15:33

1988		
Lib	22	*07:56
Sco	24	*18:57
Sag	27	*02:16
Cap	29	*05:59
Aqu	1	*07:29
Pis	3	*08:33
Ari	5	*10:37
Tau	7	*14:27
Gem	9	*20:16
Can	12	*04:08
Leo	14	*14:11
Vir	17	*02:17
Lib	19	*15:21
Sco	22	*03:12

1989		
Aqu	21	*16:56
Pis	23	*21:35
Ari	26	*01:05
Tau	28	*03:44
Gem	30	*06:08
Can	2	*09:19
Leo	4	*14:38
Vir	6	*23:05
Lib	9	*10:30
Sco	11	*23:08
Sag	14	*10:30
Cap	16	*19:00
Aqu	19	*00:34
Pis	21	*04:06

69 Cancer – Finding Your Moon Sign ☽

1990			1991			1992			1993			1994		
Can	22	*17:09	Sco	21	*17:18	Ari	23	*04:02	Leo	22	*08:25	Sag	21	*07:32
Leo	24	*18:24	Sag	24	*04:16	Tau	25	*13:27	Vir	24	*11:17	Cap	23	*08:37
Vir	26	*22:43	Cap	26	*16:49	Gem	27	*19:13	Lib	26	*13:45	Aqu	25	*11:10
Lib	29	*06:47	Aqu	29	*05:47	Can	29	*21:41	Sco	28	*16:37	Pis	27	*16:44
Sco	1	*18:00	Pis	1	*17:50	Leo	1	*22:14	Sag	30	*20:28	Ari	30	*02:07
Sag	4	*06:35	Ari	4	*03:32	Vir	3	*22:37	Cap	3	*01:49	Tau	2	*14:23
Cap	6	*18:39	Tau	6	*09:50	Lib	6	*00:28	Aqu	5	*09:14	Gem	5	*03:11
Aqu	9	*05:06	Gem	8	*12:40	Sco	8	*04:53	Pis	7	*19:09	Can	7	*14:16
Pis	11	*13:28	Can	10	*13:02	Sag	10	*12:18	Ari	10	*07:11	Leo	9	*22:42
Ari	13	*19:35	Leo	12	*12:35	Cap	12	*22:16	Tau	12	*19:36	Vir	12	*04:47
Tau	15	*23:27	Vir	14	*13:12	Aqu	15	*10:02	Gem	15	*06:06	Lib	14	*09:14
Gem	18	*01:31	Lib	16	*16:34	Pis	17	*22:44	Can	17	*13:06	Sco	16	*12:34
Can	20	*02:43	Sco	18	*23:41	Ari	20	*11:06	Leo	19	*16:46	Sag	18	*15:09
Leo	22	*04:28	Sag	21	*10:17	Tau	22	*21:34	Vir	21	*18:23	Cap	20	*17:30
												Aqu	22	*20:38

♋ Cancer – Finding Your Moon Sign ☽

1995			1996			1997			1998			1999			2000		
Tau	22	*11:36	Vir	21	*12:06	Aqu	22	*22:20	Gem	21	*21:26	Sco	23	*07:18	Pis	22	*07:5-
Gem	25	*00:02	Lib	23	*23:36	Pis	25	*00:09	Can	23	*23:39	Sag	25	*19:50	Ari	24	*17:55
Can	27	*12:55	Sco	26	*07:52	Ari	27	*02:38	Leo	26	*04:04	Cap	28	*08:11	Tau	27	*00:17
Leo	30	*01:01	Sag	28	*11:59	Tau	29	*06:23	Vir	28	*11:55	Aqu	30	*19:19	Gem	29	*02:53
Vir	2	*11:34	Cap	30	*12:46	Gem	1	*11:35	Lib	30	*23:05	Pis	3	*04:34	Can	1	*03:09
Lib	4	*19:54	Aqu	2	*12:05	Can	3	*18:32	Sco	3	*11:44	Ari	5	*11:20	Leo	3	*02:38
Sco	7	*01:17	Pis	4	*12:07	Leo	6	*03:45	Sag	5	*23:22	Tau	7	*15:21	Vir	5	*03:19
Sag	9	*03:36	Ari	6	*14:42	Vir	8	*15:21	Cap	8	*08:26	Gem	9	*16:59	Lib	7	*06:46
Cap	11	*03:43	Tau	8	*20:44	Lib	11	*04:20	Aqu	10	*14:51	Can	11	*17:27	Sco	9	*13:49
Aqu	13	*03:21	Gem	11	*05:52	Sco	13	*16:19	Pis	12	*19:22	Leo	13	*18:25	Sag	12	*00:C6
Pis	15	*04:37	Can	13	*17:07	Sag	16	*01:00	Ari	14	*22:44	Vir	15	*21:39	Cap	14	*12:27
Ari	17	*09:24	Leo	16	*05:31	Cap	18	*05:45	Tau	17	*01:33	Lib	18	*04:19	Aqu	17	*01:26
Tau	19	*18:20	Vir	18	*18:16	Aqu	20	*07:28	Gem	19	*04:18	Sco	20	*14:30	Pis	19	*13:43
Gem	22	*06:23	Lib	21	*06:13	Pis	22	*07:59	Can	21	*07:43				Ari	22	*00:08

♋ Cancer Mercury Signs ☿

YEAR	GEMINI	CANCER	LEO
1930	21 Jun–4 Jul	4 Jul–19 Jul	19 Jul–23 Jul
1931	21 Jun–26 Jun	26 Jun–10 Jul	10 Jul–23 Jul
1932		21 Jun–2 Jul	2 Jul–23 Jul
1933		21 Jun–27 Jun	27 Jun–23 Jul
1934		21 Jun–23 Jul	
1935	21 Jun–13 Jul	13 Jul–23 Jul	
1936	21 Jun–8 Jul	8 Jul–23 Jul	
1937	21 Jun–1 Jul	1 Jul–15 Jul	15 Jul–23 Jul
1938	22 Jun	22 Jun–7 Jul	7 Jul–23 Jul
1939		22 Jun–30 Jun	30 Jun–23 Jul
1940		21 Jun–26 Jun	26 Jun–21 Jul
		21 Jul–23 Jul	
1941		21 Jun–23 Jul	
1942	21 Jun–12 Jul	12 Jul–23 Jul	
1943	21 Jun–6 Jul	6 Jul–20 Jul	20 Jul–23 Jul
1944	21 Jun–27 Jun	27 Jun–11 Jul	11 Jul–23 Jul
1945		21 Jun–3 Jul	3 Jul–23 Jul
1946		21 Jun–27 Jun	27 Jun–23 Jul
1947		21 Jun–23 Jul	
1948	28 Jun–11 Jul	21 Jun–28 Jun	
		11 Jul–23 Jul	
1949	21 Jun–10 Jul	10 Jul–23 Jul	
1950	21 Jun–2 Jul	2 Jul–16 Jul	16 Jul–23 Jul
1951	21 Jun–24 Jun	24 Jun–8 Jul	8 Jul–23 Jul
1952		21 Jun–30 Jun	30 Jun–23 Jul
1953		21 Jun–26 Jun	26 Jun–23 Jul
1954		21 Jun–23 Jul	
1955	21 Jun–13 Jul	13 Jul–23 Jul	
1956	21 Jun–6 Jul	6 Jul–21 Jul	21 Jul–23 Jul

YEAR	GEMINI	CANCER	LEO
1957	21 Jun–28 Jun	28 Jun–12 Jul	12 Jul–23 Jul
1958		21 Jun–4 Jul	4 Jul–23 Jul
1959		21 Jun–28 Jun	28 Jun–23 Jul
1960		21 Jun–1 Jul	1 Jul–6 Jul
		6 Jul–23 Jul	
1961		21 Jun–23 Jul	
1962	21 Jun–11 Jul	11 Jul–23 Jul	
1963	21 Jun–4 Jul	4 Jul–18 Jul	18 Jul–23 Jul
1964	21 Jun–24 Jun	24 Jun–9 Jul	9 Jul–23 Jul
1965		21 Jun–1 Jul	1 Jul–23 Jul
1966		21 Jun–26 Jun	26 Jun–23 Jul
1967		21 Jun–23 Jul	
1968	21 Jun–13 Jul	13 Jul–23 Jul	
1969	21 Jun–8 Jul	8 Jul–22 Jul	22 Jul–23 Jul
1970	21 Jun–30 Jun	30 Jun–14 Jul	14 Jul–23 Jul
1971		21 Jun–6 Jul	6 Jul–23 Jul
1972		21 Jun–28 Jun	28 Jun–23 Jul
1973		21 Jun–27 Jun	27 Jun–16 Jul
		16 Jul–23 Jul	
1974		21 Jun–23 Jul	
1975	21 Jun–12 Jul	12 Jul–23 Jul	
1976	21 Jun–4 Jul	4 Jul–18 Jul	18 Jul–23 Jul
1977	21 Jun–26 Jun	26 Jun–10 Jul	10 Jul–23 Jul
1978		21 Jun–2 Jul	2 Jul–23 Jul
1979		21 Jun–27 Jun	27 Jun–23 Jul
1980		21 Jun–23 Jul	
1981	22 Jun–12 Jul	21 Jun–22 Jun	
		12 Jul–23 Jul	
1982	21 Jun–9 Jul	9 Jul–23 Jul	
1983	21 Jun–1 Jul	1 Jul–15 Jul	15 Jul–23 Jul
1984	21–22 Jun	22 Jun–6 Jul	6 Jul–23 Jul
1985		21 Jun–29 Jun	29 Jun–23 Jul

YEAR	GEMINI	CANCER	LEO
1986		21 Jun–26 Jun	26 Jun–23 Jul
1987		21 Jun–23 Jul	
1988	21 Jun–12 Jul	12 Jul–23 Jul	
1989	21 Jun–6 Jul	6 Jul–20 Jul	20 Jul–23 Jul
1990	21 Jun–27 Jun	27 Jun–11 Jul	11 Jul–23 Jul
1991		21 Jun–4 Jul	4 Jul–23 Jul
1992		21 Jun–27 Jun	27 Jun–23 Jul
1993		21 Jun–23 Jul	
1994	2 Jul–10 Jul	21 Jun–2 Jul	
		10 Jul–23 Jul	
1995	21 Jun–10 Jul	10 Jul–23 Jul	
1996	21 Jun–2 Jul	2 Jul–16 Jul	16 Jul–23 Jul
1997	21 Jun–23 Jun	23 Jun–8 Jul	8 Jul–23 Jul
1998		21 Jun–30 Jun	30 Jun–23 Jul
1999		21 Jun–26 Jun	26 Jun–23 Jul
2000		21 Jun–23 Jul	

69 Cancer Venus Signs ♀

YEAR	TAURUS	GEMINI	CANCER	LEO	VIRGO
1930		21 Jun–9 Jul / 13 Jul–23 Jul	9 Jul–23 Jul / 21 Jun–13 Jul	21 Jun–14 Jul	14 Jul–23 Jul
1931					
1932			21 Jun–3 Jul		
1933		28 Jun–23 Jul		3 Jul–23 Jul	
1934	21 Jun–28 Jun				7 Jul–23 Jul
1935		21 Jun–23 Jun / 7 Jul–23 Jul		21 Jun–7 Jul / 17 Jul–23 Jul	
1936	21 Jun–7 Jul		23 Jun–17 Jul		
1937				21 Jun–14 Jul	14 Jul–23 Jul
1938		21 Jun–9 Jul	9 Jul–23 Jul / 21 Jun–5 Jul / 21 Jun–2 Jul		
1939				5 Jul–23 Jul / 2 Jul–23 Jul	
1940					
1941					
1942	21 Jun–27 Jun	27 Jun–23 Jul		21 Jun–7 Jul / 17 Jul–23 Jul	7 Jul–23 Jul
1943			22 Jun–17 Jul		
1944	21 Jun–7 Jul	21–22 Jun / 7 Jul–23 Jul			
1945					
1946		21 Jun–8 Jul		21 Jun–13 Jul	13 Jul–23 Jul
1947			8 Jul–23 Jul / 21 Jun–29 Jun / 1 Jul–23 Jul / 23 Jul		
1948				29 Jun–23 Jul	
1949		21 Jun–1 Jul / 27 Jun–23 Jul			
1950	21 Jun–27 Jun			21 Jun–8 Jul	8 Jul–23 Jul
1951					

YEAR	TAURUS	GEMINI	CANCER	LEO	VIRGO
1952		21–22 Jun	22 Jun–16 Jul	16 Jul–23 Jul	
1953	21 Jun–7 Jul	7 Jul–23 Jul			
1954				21 Jun–13 Jul	13 Jul–23 Jul
1955		21 Jun–8 Jul	8 Jul–23 Jul		
1956		23 Jun–23 Jul	21 Jun–23 Jun		
1957			21 Jun–1 Jul 23 Jul	1 Jul–23 Jul	
1958	21 Jun–26 Jun	26 Jun–23 Jul			
1959			21 Jun–16 Jul	21 Jun–8 Jul 16 Jul–23 Jul	8 Jul–23 Jul
1960					
1961	23 Jul–7 Jul	7 Jul–23 Jul	21 Jun–12 Jul 7 Jul–23 Jul	12 Jul–23 Jul	
1962		21 Jun–7 Jul			
1963		21 Jun–23 Jul			
1964			21 Jun–30 Jun 21 Jul–23 Jul	30 Jun–23 Jul	
1965		26 Jun–21 Jul	21 Jul–23 Jul		
1966	21 Jun–26 Jun			21 Jun–8 Jul 15 Jul–23 Jul	8 Jul–23 Jul
1967			21 Jun–15 Jul		
1968					
1969	21 Jun–6 Jul	6 Jul–23 Jul		21 Jun–12 Jul	
1970			6 Jul–23 Jul		12 Jul–23 Jul
1971		21 Jun–6 Jul			
1972		21 Jun–23 Jul			
1973			21 Jun–30 Jun 21 Jul–23 Jul	30 Jun–23 Jul	
1974	21 Jun–25 Jun	25 Jun–21 Jul			
1975				21 Jun–9 Jul 14 Jul–23 Jul	9 Jul–23 Jul
1976			21 Jun–14 Jul		

YEAR	TAURUS	GEMINI	CANCER	LEO	VIRGO
1977	21 Jun–6 Jul	6 Jul–23 Jul	6 Jul–23 Jul	21 Jun–12 Jul	12 Jul–23 Jul
1978					
1979		21 Jun–6 Jul	21 Jun–29 Jun	29 Jun–23 Jul	
1980		21 Jun–23 Jul	20 Jul–23 Jul		
1981					
1982	21 Jun–25 Jun	25 Jun–20 Jul	21 Jun–14 Jul	21 Jun–10 Jul	10 Jul–23 Jul
1983				14 Jul–23 Jul	
1984					
1985	21 Jun–6 Jul	6 Jul–23 Jul	5 Jul–23 Jul	21 Jun–11 Jul	11 Jul–23 Jul
1986					
1987		21 Jun–5 Jul	21 Jun–29 Jun	29 Jun–23 Jul	
1988		21 Jun–23 Jul	20 Jul–23 Jul		
1989					
1990	21 Jun–25 Jun	25 Jun–20 Jul	21 Jun–13 Jul	21 Jun–11 Jul	11 Jul–23 Jul
1991				13 Jul–23 Jul	
1992					
1993	21 Jun–6 Jul	6 Jul–23 Jul	5 Jul–23 Jul	21 Jun–11 Jul	11 Jul–23 Jul
1994					
1995		21 Jun–5 Jul	21 Jun–28 Jun	28 Jun–23 Jul	
1996		21 Jun–23 Jul	19 Jul–23 Jul		
1997					
1998	21 Jun–24 Jun	24 Jun–19 Jul	21 Jun–13 Jul	21 Jun–12 Jul	12 Jul–23 Jul
1999				13 Jul–23 Jul	
2000					

118

The Cancer Workbook

There are no right or wrong answers in this chapter. Its aim is to help you assess how you are doing with your life – in YOUR estimation – and to make the material of this book more personal and, I hope, more helpful for you.

1. The Cancer in You
Which of the following Cancer characteristics do you recognise in yourself?

creative	imaginative	intuitive
nurturing	supportive	resourceful
family-focused	romantic	sympathetic
tender	understanding	sensitive

2. In which situations do you find yourself acting like this?

_____

_____

3. When you are feeling vulnerable you may show some of the less constructive Cancer traits. Do you recognise yourself in any of the following?

blaming	childish	clannish
clingy	defensive	manipulative
moody	resentful	irrational

What kind of situations trigger off this behaviour and what do you think might help you, in these situations, to respond more positively?

_____

_____

4. You and Your Roles
a) Where in your life do you play the role of Nurturer?

_____

_____

b) Whom, or what, do you nurture?

_____

_____

5. Do you play any of the following roles – in the literal or broad sense – in any part of your life? If not, would you like to? What might be your first step towards doing so?

Creator   Intuitive   Provider
Recluse   Nest-Builder   Historian

_____

_____

6. Sun Aspects
If any of the following planets aspects your Sun, add each of the keywords for that planet to complete the following sentences. Which phrases ring true for you?

I am _____

My father is _____

My job requires that I am _____

Saturn Words (Use only if your Sun is aspected by Saturn)

ambitious	controlling	judgmental	mature
serious	strict	traditional	bureaucratic
cautious	committed	hard-working	disciplined
depressive	responsible	status-seeking	limiting

Uranus Words (Use only if your Sun is aspected by Uranus)

freedom-loving	progressive	rebellious	shocking
scientific	cutting-edge	detached	contrary
friendly	disruptive	eccentric	humanitarian
innovative	nonconformist	unconventional	exciting

Neptune Words (Use only if your Sun is aspected by Neptune)

sensitive	idealistic	artistic	impressionable
disappointing	impractical	escapist	self-sacrificing
spiritual	unrealistic	dreamy	glamorous
dependent	deceptive	rescuing	blissful

Pluto Words (Use only if your Sun is aspected by Pluto)

powerful	single-minded	intense	extreme
secretive	rotten	passionate	mysterious
investigative	uncompromising	ruthless	wealthy
abusive	regenerative	associated with sex, birth or death	

a) If one or more negative words describe you or your job, how might you turn that quality into something more positive or satisfying?

_____

_____

7. The Moon and You

Below are brief lists of what the Moon needs, in the various elements, to feel secure and satisfied. First find your Moon element, then estimate how much of each of the following you are expressing and receiving in your life, especially at home and in your relationships, on a scale of 0 to 5 where 0 = none and 5 = plenty.

FIRE MOONS — Aries, Leo, Sagittarius

attention	action	drama
recognition	self-expression	spontaneity
enthusiasm	adventure	leadership

EARTH MOONS — Taurus, Virgo, Capricorn

stability	orderly routine	sensual pleasures
material security	a sense of rootedness	control over your home life
regular body care	practical achievements	pleasurable practical tasks

AIR MOONS — Gemini, Libra, Aquarius

mental rapport	stimulating ideas	emotional space
friendship	social justice	interesting conversations
fairness	socialising	freedom to circulate

WATER MOONS — Cancer, Scorpio, Pisces

intimacy	a sense of belonging	emotional rapport
emotional safety	respect for your feelings	time and space to retreat
acceptance	cherishing and being cherished	warmth and comfort

a) Do you feel your Moon is being 'fed' enough?

yes_____no _____

b) How might you satisfy your Moon needs even better?

_____

_____

8. You and Your Mercury

As a Cancerian, your Mercury can only be in Gemini, Cancer or Leo. Below are some of the ways and situations in which Mercury in each of the elements might learn and communicate effectively. First find your Mercury sign, then circle the words you think apply to you.

Mercury in Fire (Leo)

action	imagination	identifying with the subject matter
excitement	drama	playing with possibilities

Mercury in Earth (As a Cancer, you can never have Mercury in an earth sign; the words are included here for completeness)

time-tested methods	useful facts	well-structured information
'how to' instructions	demonstrations	hands-on experience

Mercury in Air (Gemini)

facts arranged in categories	logic	demonstrable connections
rational arguments	theories	debate and sharing of ideas

Mercury in Water (Cancer)

pictures and images	charged atmospheres	feeling-linked information
intuitive understanding	emotional rapport	being shown personally

a) This game with Mercury can be done with a friend or on your own. Skim through a magazine until you find a picture that interests you. Then describe the picture – to your friend, or in writing or on tape. Notice what you emphasise and the kind of words you use. Now try to describe it using the language and emphasis of each of the other Mercury modes. How easy did you find that? Identifying the preferred Mercury style of others and using that style yourself can lead to improved communication all round.

9. Your Venus Values
Below are lists of qualities and situations that your Venus sign might enjoy. Assess on a scale of 0 to 5 how much your Venus desires and pleasures are met and expressed in your life. 0 = not at all, 5 = fully.

Venus in Taurus
You will activate your Venus through whatever pleases the senses and enhances your sense of stability, for example:

financial security	beauty	gardening and nature
sensual pleasures	good food	body pampering

Venus in Gemini
You will activate your Venus through anything that stimulates your mind and uses a talent for making connections, for example:

playing go-between	flirting	talking and writing
passing on new ideas	witty use of words	trend-spotting

Venus in Cancer

You will activate your Venus through anything that makes you feel wise, intuitive, nurturing and nurtured, and at the centre of a 'family', for example:

a beautiful home	tenderness	sharing meals with loved ones
sharing feelings safely	home comforts	your family or country history

Venus in Leo

You will activate your Venus through anything that makes you feel special, unique, radiant and generous, for example:

extravagant gestures	luxury goods	prestigious activities
being central in a drama	acting nobly	being in love

Venus in Virgo

You will activate your Venus through anything that engages your powers of discrimination, for example:

restoring order	improving efficiency	using your skills
purifying your mind, body or environment	being of service	quality work

a) How, and where, might you have more fun and pleasure by bringing more of what your Venus sign loves into your life?

_____

_____

b) Make a note here of the kind of gifts your Venus sign would love to receive. Then go on and spoil yourself . . .

_____

_____

Resources

Finding an Astrologer

I'm often asked what is the best way to find a reputable astrologer. Personal recommendation by someone whose judgement you trust is by far the best way. Ideally, the astrologer should also be endorsed by a reputable organisation whose members adhere to a strict code of ethics, which guarantees confidentiality and professional conduct.

Contact Addresses

Association of Professional Astrologers
www.professionalastrologers.org
    APA members adhere to a strict code of professional ethics.

Astrological Association of Great Britain
www.astrologicalassociation.co.uk
    The main body for astrology in the UK that also has information on astrological events and organisations throughout the world.

Faculty of Astrological Studies
www.astrology.org.uk
    The teaching body internationally recognised for excellence in astrological education at all levels.

Your Cancerian Friends

You can keep a record of Cancerians you know here, with the page numbers of where to find their descriptions handy for future reference.

Name _____ Date of Birth _____

Aspects★	None	Saturn	Uranus	Neptune	Pluto

Moon Sign _____ p _____

Mercury Sign _____ p _____

Venus Sign _____ p _____

Name _____ Date of Birth _____

Aspects★	None	Saturn	Uranus	Neptune	Pluto

Moon Sign _____ p _____

Mercury Sign _____ p _____

Venus Sign _____ p _____

Name _____ Date of Birth _____

Aspects★	None	Saturn	Uranus	Neptune	Pluto

Moon Sign _____ p _____

Mercury Sign _____ p _____

Venus Sign _____ p _____

Name _____ Date of Birth _____

Aspects★	None	Saturn	Uranus	Neptune	Pluto

Moon Sign _____ p _____

Mercury Sign _____ p _____

Venus Sign _____ p _____

★ Circle where applicable

Sign Summaries

SIGN	GLYPH	APPROX DATES	SYMBOL	ROLE	ELEMENT	QUALITY	PLANET	GLYPH	KEYWORD
1. Aries	♈	21/3 – 19/4	Ram	Hero	Fire	Cardinal	Mars	♂	Assertiveness
2. Taurus	♉	20/4 – 20/5	Bull	Steward	Earth	Fixed	Venus	♀	Stability
3. Gemini	♊	21/5 – 21/6	Twins	Go-Between	Air	Mutable	Mercury	☿	Communication
4. Cancer	♋	22/6 – 22/7	Crab	Caretaker	Water	Cardinal	Moon	☽	Nurture
5. Leo	♌	23/7 – 22/8	Lion	Performer	Fire	Fixed	Sun	☉	Glory
6. Virgo	♍	23/8 – 22/9	Maiden	Craftworker	Earth	Mutable	Mercury	☿	Skill
7. Libra	♎	23/9 – 22/10	Scales	Architect	Air	Cardinal	Venus	♀	Balance
8. Scorpio	♏	23/10 – 23/11	Scorpion	Survivor	Water	Fixed	Pluto	♇	Transformation
9. Sagittarius	♐	22/11 – 21/12	Archer	Adventurer	Fire	Mutable	Jupiter	♃	Wisdom
10. Capricorn	♑	22/12 – 19/1	Goat	Manager	Earth	Cardinal	Saturn	♄	Responsibility
11. Aquarius	♒	20/1 – 19/2	Waterbearer	Scientist	Air	Fixed	Uranus	♅	Progress
12. Pisces	♓	20/2 – 20/3	Fishes	Dreamer	Water	Mutable	Neptune	♆	Universality

Annie Dalton

Illustrated by Laura Clark
& Kris Stoddart

A & C Black • London

White Wor
Centre for Liter

This book can be used in the Whi
programme by more advanced r

First paperback edition 2012
First published in hardback in 2012 by
A & C Black
Bloomsbury Publishing Plc
50 Bedford Square
London
WC1B 3DP

www.acblack.com

ISBN 978-1-4081-3949-3

A CIP catalogue for this book is available from the British Library.

Chapter 1

The boy was sitting next to an old stone
fountain in the marketplace. He had come to
the city to find food but all he'd found was a
stray puppy. He picked it up to keep it safe.

The city was a cruel and frightening place. Above the rooftops the sky was red and smoky. People were running and shouting. Buildings were burning.

The boy longed for a drink of water but the fountain was broken. "Everything in this city is broken," he thought. "And not just this city. Everything in the world."

He closed his eyes and pictured his dad's workshop. Sometimes his dad used to let him do simple things like smoothing down the rough wood with a plane. The boy could almost smell the wood-shavings. He quickly opened his eyes. The smell of wood was real!

6

An old man was pushing a cart full of freshly cut planks. He wasn't looking at the burning buildings. He just kept walking, pushing his squeaky old cart.

"That's Nutty Noah!" one of the street
kids told the boy. "He says God told him the
world is ending. He's building a boat for his
family to sail away in." He picked up a stone
to throw at the old man.

8

"Don't!" The boy knocked the stone out of the street kid's hand and ran after the old man. "Mr Noah! Wait!"

The old man turned.

"I want to help you build the boat," the boy said shyly.

The old man smiled. "Then come with me."

Chapter 2

They hurried along until they reached a pair of tall gates. Noah unlocked the gates and the boy followed him into a large courtyard piled high with wood.

Inside Noah's family were sitting down to eat.

"This boy is going to help me build the Ark," Noah told his wife, smiling.

Mrs Noah didn't smile back. "I suppose God told you to bring him!" she grumbled. "Two extra mouths to feed!"

11

Noah's granddaughter Martha brought food for the boy and his dog. "I'm glad you've come," she said. "Now Grandpa's boat might be ready in time."

The boy swallowed. "You mean before the world ends?"

Mrs Noah gave a scornful laugh. "The world will still be here next year, and we'll have a stupid great boat in our back garden!"

That night the boy couldn't sleep. He
peeped over the edge of the roof and saw
Noah walking in the garden. He seemed to
be talking to someone. The moon was as
thin as a fingernail, yet the garden was full
of light. The boy shivered as he understood.
Noah was talking to God.

Chapter 3

Next morning, Noah and his three sons started to saw the planks. The boy helped to sand them smooth.

14

The boy was amazed when he saw the plans for the Ark. It didn't look like a boat. It looked like a tiny town. "Why do you need so much room?" he asked.

"The Ark isn't just for my family," Noah explained. "It's for the animals."

"Which animals?"

"The animals are the reason God told Grandpa to build the ark," said Martha. "It will keep them safe until the Earth is fit to live on again."

"How are you going to fit them all inside?" asked the boy.

"We won't have to, silly. God is only sending us two of every kind," Martha said.

Mrs Noah had come out with bread and cheese for their lunch. She gave her scornful laugh. "And where are all these animals coming from, does anybody know?"

"We haven't got time to eat," Noah told his wife. "We must work while there's still light."

Chapter 4

They started work at dawn and they kept working until the first stars came out. Noah said they were running out of time.

Then, one evening, as the sun was setting over the burning city, Noah laid down his hammer. "It's finished!" he said.

That night the city was quiet, but the boy couldn't sleep. Suppose the animals didn't come? He watched a small cloud drift in front of the moon. "Perhaps it will rain," he thought. It hadn't rained for months.

Just before dawn Martha woke him. She took him to the edge of the roof and the boy looked down over the sleeping city.

"They're here," he whispered.

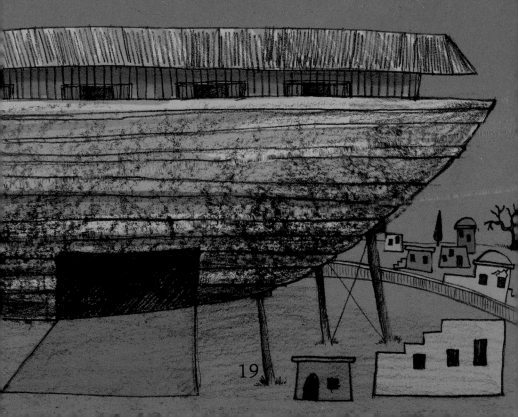

19

A strange procession was winding through the streets towards them. Some creatures padded along, some trotted, some fluttered and flew. The boy recognised camels, donkeys, chickens, elephants, wolves, tigers, crocodiles. Some beasts he only knew from stories.

Noah and his wife came to watch with them. Mrs Noah took her husband's hand. "I'm sorry," she told him. "You were right and I was wrong."

20

High above the city, thunder clouds were piling up. The boy saw a flash of lightning. "Run and open the gates!" Mrs Noah told the children. "There isn't much time!"

21

Chapter 5

The boy wondered if angels were guiding the birds and animals, they were so calm and peaceful. They made their way to the lower decks of the Ark and settled in the straw.

By the time the last animals had come on board, the first rain-drops were falling. Noah and his sons just had time to fasten the doors and windows.

Then the storm struck.

It didn't sound like wind and rain, it sounded as if soldiers were attacking the Ark with hammers, trying to break it apart. The puppy shivered in the boy's arms. Martha had her hands over her ears, trying to shut out the noise.

Suddenly they felt themselves being lifted up and up, and next minute they were swept away with the flood.

Chapter 6

It felt as if they were sailing through an endless night.

Outside, the wind howled and the rain hammered. Inside, the boy helped to take care of the animals and made sure the Ark didn't spring any leaks.

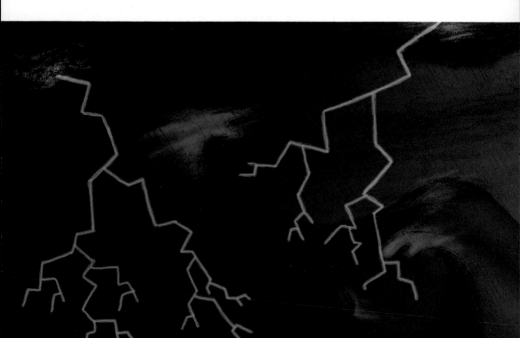

One day they woke to complete silence. The storm had stopped.

Noah started taking the boards down from the windows. Outside they saw rain-clouds above a shining sheet of water that seemed to stretch on forever. There was nothing left on the Earth except for the creatures inside the Ark. Everything else was far below, drowned.

The next day, the sun appeared. Everyone went up to enjoy the pale watery rays. "It's so quiet," thought the boy. There was no birdsong, no leaves rustling, just the slap of water against the Ark, and the sound of their own breathing.

One morning, before dawn, the Ark stopped moving. The children dashed up on deck and saw that they had come to rest on a hill top. Their long voyage was over.

For months the Ark had been their home. They had been too busy taking care of the animals to worry about what would happen next. Now, suddenly, they were afraid.

Noah told the children to bring him two birds. They ran down to the lower deck and brought back a raven and a dove.

"Release them," said Noah. "If there is anything green and growing, the birds will find it."

They watched the birds fly away until they looked like tiny dots. Then even the dots disappeared.

All that day and the next, they waited.
On the third day, as the sun was setting, the
boy heard the soft whirr of wings. The dove
had returned alone. In her beak was a sprig
of olive. The Earth was coming back to life.

A few days later, Noah opened up the Ark and released the birds and animals into a wet and sparkling new world.

At the same moment a beautiful rainbow appeared shimmering overhead. Noah told them that the rainbow was God's sign that He would never harm the Earth again.

31

"This time, things will be different," the boy thought. "This time, people will take care of each other and their planet."

"Race you!" the boy said to Martha. With the puppy chasing after them, they sprinted across the plank and on to dry land.